P9-DYJ-544

Life,
Love,
Church,
and
Other
Dangerous
Idols

SEDUCTION
OF THE LESSER
GODS

Life,
Love,
Church,
and
Other
Dangerous
Idols

SEDUCTION
OF THE LESSER
GODS

LESLIE WILLIAMS

WORD PUBLISHING
Nashville·London·Vancouver·Melbourne

PUBLISHED BY WORD PUBLISHING
Nashville, Tennessee

Seduction of the Lesser Gods: Life, Love, Church, and other dangerous idols.
Copyright © 1997 by Leslie Williams. All rights reserved. No portion
of this book may be reproduced, stored in a retrieval system, or trans-
mitted in any form or by any means—electronic, mechanical, photo-
copy, recording, or any other—except for brief quotations in printed
reviews, without the prior permission of the publisher.

Unless otherwise noted, Scripture quotations are from the Revised
Standard Version of the Bible (RSV). Copyright © 1946, 1952, 1971,
1973 by the Division of Christian Education of the National Council
of Churches of Christ in the U.S.A. Used by permission.

Scripture quotations noted AB are from The Amplified Bible: Old Testament. Copyright © 1962, 1964 by Zondervan Publishing House
(used by permission); and from The Amplified New Testament. Copyright © 1958 by the Lockman Foundation (used by permission).

Library of Congress Cataloging-in-Publication Data

Williams, Leslie.
    Seduction of the lesser gods: life, love, church, and other
dangerous idols / by Leslie Williams.
    p.   cm.
Includes bibliographical references.
ISBN 0-8499-1491-4
    1. Christian life.   2. Idolatry.   I. Title.
BV4627.I34.W55   1998
248.4–dc21   97-44340
                                                                 CIP

Printed in the United States of America
8 0 1 2 3 4 9 QBP 9 8 7 6 5 4 3 2 1

To Jase and Caroline

TABLE OF CONTENTS

ACKNOWLEDGMENTS

I would like to thank my husband, Stockton Williams, for a variety of things: his insightful comments about the original manuscript, his patience with my deadlines, and his continued love and support. My children, Jase and Caroline, too, deserve much thanks for loaning out their mom for various writing events and for their willingness to eat lots of frozen pizza.

Special thanks goes to Mary-Allen Meriwether and Angela Hock for their excellent editorial comments, to Mary-Keith Dickinson for her wise suggestions, and to my Education for Ministry group for their insights and prayers during the writing of this book. I am especially grateful to my in-laws: Mary Pearl Williams; Jim and Shelley Austin; and Stephanie and Larry Laden for their love and support. Thanks also to Bill Gohring for his continued encouragement and expertise in the book business. Finally, I'd like to thank the great team at Word for their advice, friendship, and superb professionalism.

Chapter 1

THE LESSER GODS

*O senseless man who cannot make a worm,
and yet makes gods by dozens.*

—MICHEL DE MONTAIGNE

They were quite a pair, the old cheat Laban and his son-in-law, Jacob the trickster. They lived close by for many years, each trying to get the better of the other, until one night an angel swooped down to Jacob in a dream and told him to go home. In his typical deceitful style, Jacob didn't announce his plans, pack up, throw one last good-bye party, and head out. Instead, he waited until Laban was off shearing sheep, then skulked out across the desert at night. Though his household must have made a ruckus for miles, Jacob escaped in secret with his wives, children, camels, cattle, and goats.

To further this story already riddled with deception, Rachel, too, became a sneak. Without telling either her husband or her father, she stole Laban's household gods on the way out the door.

Three days later, trouble hit. Laban returned home and discovered Jacob and his household had fled. Purple with rage, he thundered after them into the hill country, railing about how he'd been cheated. The final showdown between Jacob and Laban ended in a shaky truce, but they agreed on one thing: to kill the person who stole Laban's household gods. And so began an all-out search.

In the meantime, Rachel stuffed the household gods in her saddlebag and perched on top of her camel while her father ransacked the tents. She begged off, claiming that she couldn't get down because "the way of women" (Gen. 31:35) was upon her, meaning either that she was in her period or that she was already pregnant with Benjamin. The household gods thus remained hidden under her skirts; and Rachel, it turned out, temporarily got the best of both men.

LITTLE MOONS AND LESSER GODS

Early on, this incident snagged my attention. My childhood Bible has a big blue question mark in the margin beside "and Rachel stole her father's household gods." What were these lesser gods? Why were they so important that Rachel stole them, lied about them to her husband and her father, then risked her life to keep them?

Later I learned that the household gods were a sign of inheritance. By stealing them, Rachel became the favored child, even over her brothers. These small clay figurines symbolized the spirit of the house and were supposed to bring blessings. The person who claimed the household gods inherited the strength of the family.

Yet a deeper question still rankled: If Jacob and Rachel were our patriarchs in the true faith, why was she interested in petty household gods at all, when Yahweh Himself was her protector and the great dispenser of blessings? Why settle for lesser gods when you can worship God Almighty?

Later on in the saga of Jacob and Rachel, the situation becomes even more complicated. After Shechem ravishes Jacob's daughter Dinah and Jacob punishes the Hivites in retaliation, God tells Jacob to go to Bethel and make an altar there. At this point (Gen. 35:2), Jacob instructs his household to put away all foreign gods. What the Bible doesn't say is whether Rachel obeyed him or not. The next thing we hear is that Rachel dies in childbirth after heavy travail.

Some people have interpreted her death as punishment for taking the household gods from her father. She was not blessed, as she had expected. But the question for us today is this: What can we all learn from Rachel? What do these lesser gods have to do with our lives?

Though I certainly don't worship little clay statuettes tucked into a niche in our kitchen, I have a host of lesser gods to which I unwittingly, almost unconsciously, pay homage. Like most practicing Christians, I've been taught not to worship the obvious idols like money, fame, and power. Those are such well-known sins that no good clergyman's wife would admit to committing them—though escaping unscathed from their clutches is nearly an impossible task (and another story). No, the lesser gods I'm talking about are things like love, safety, service, accomplishment, understanding, goodness—even life itself. Most of these radiate virtue and goodness and seem like harmless decorative items in a spiritual life. But when sought after for themselves, these lesser gods are dust compared to the breath of real life offered by Jesus Christ. The nature of an idol is that it looks great—irresistibly great—but can't deliver.

Like little moons, these lesser gods orbit our personal universes. They do not generate happiness, light, and life of themselves, as Jesus does. Instead they reflect the light of the Generator of all light.

Love, goodness, and sacrifice for Christ are not bad things, of course. However, they are gifts, by-products of a life lived in Christ. They are blessings lavishly bestowed by a loving God on His children.

The heart of my spiritual journey has been a process of recognizing one by one how I've misjudged the pale reflective light of these good things, mistaking the lesser glow for the light of the living Christ. Bit by bit, I've recognized how the danger comes when we seek them instead of seeking Jesus. To confuse the gift for the giver is a fatal spiritual mistake.

For example, in 1984, I underwent major surgery for endometriosis. My husband, Stockton, and I had been trying unsuccessfully for almost five years to conceive or adopt a child, and my prayer life had become one long plea for a baby. That spring of 1984, the surgery went well, and I lay in the hospital bed drinking cranberry juice and eating jello with high hopes.

Later, when it was apparent the surgery hadn't worked, I received a present in the mail—a mug from a well-meaning friend who had, unfortunately, been particularly insensitive to my plight. The mug was decorated in blue with the words from Psalm 37: "Delight in the Lord, and he shall give you your heart's desire." I'm sure the gift was intended to cheer me up, to give me hope after my operation.

The effect, of course, was the opposite. Not only did I not delight in the Lord—I was angry at God for denying my request—but it seemed as though He had gone out of His way to take away my heart's desire. Again. Psalm 37 was an indictment of my faith. By giving me the mug, my friend, pregnant at the time with twins, seemed to be giving me the message: "Look at me. I had faith and God rewarded me." The implication was that my faith was not strong enough because God had not given me my heart's desire.

I threw the mug in the trash.

The "gift" hurt so much that it got stuck in my craw for several years, and every time I heard that verse, I felt like crying. As my husband and I continued to struggle with infertility, I continued to struggle with that verse. My spiritual crisis was somehow tied in with that verse, and with not having a baby.

Maybe I wasn't truly delighting in the Lord. Every month, it became more and more difficult to delight in a God who seemed to rob me of what every other woman I knew achieved so effortlessly. Or maybe my desire was out of line. Was asking for a baby too much? Was I being greedy?

Maybe I shouldn't want a baby at all. After two more years and my third surgery, I simply begged God to take away all desire for a child. If I didn't want a baby in the first place, I wouldn't be so bitterly disappointed every month.

Though it took almost seven years, I finally realized the problem lay not in the desire for a child, but in the fact that I desired a child more than I desired God's will for my life. I needed to bring my desire in line with God's desire— only then could I truly delight in Him. If God wanted me to be childless (for whatever reason, whether I understood it or not), then I needed to desire what He wanted.

The first blessing He gave me was forgiveness for my idolatry and lack of faith. The great river of peace came later, but when I finally recognized the problem, the "rightness" of relationship began to trickle in. At first it was a queasy sort of acceptance, a tentative relief broken only occasionally by bouts of sadness, but a great improvement over the anguish of the previous seven years. My childlessness no longer separated me from God's love.

The second blessing was two beautiful, brilliant, adorable children He gave us through the Gladney Center in Fort Worth. When I relinquished what I thought was my heart's desire, He first (over time), filled my heart with Himself and His love—and then gave me babies more perfect and wonderful than Stockton and I could possibly have produced on our own.

Even though I knew better, I had fallen victim to the God-as-a-vending-machine syndrome: You drop your prayers in like quarters, and He gives you the goodie you want. Dangerous and sloppy theology. We are called to want God more than His blessings, and when we focus on what God can (or doesn't) give us, we lose our bearings.

Always, the redemption is greater than the sacrifice. We give up what we think we want, and inevitably, He fills us with more good things than the poverty of our imagination allows. We just have to remember that the process is not like making instant Kool-Aid, but like the aging of fine wine. It takes lots of time, and grace.

THE SUBTLE POWER OF THE LESSER GODS

Kurt was a young seminarian. Three days after the exam results were mailed, Kurt spotted his letter behind the cracked glass of cubicle 27, fifth down and two over in the wall of post office boxes guarding the student lounge like a columbarium. The other Episcopal seminary students had already received their results of the national General Ordination Exams. Typical. Kurt's ordination track had been filled with potholes and obstacles—committees who weren't happy with his grades, a bishop who thought he was too sure of himself, and a wife who had cried nightly the first year away from home. He needed to pass all seven areas on the national test, areas such as theology, Bible, pastoral care—or the bishop would not ordain him. Yet he was confident; he'd been called by God, and God was higher than the bishop.

Feeling suddenly damp around the armpits, Kurt clicked the combination lock and missed his final number. Angrily he spun the dial again, and this time the tiny door squeaked open. The letter lay on top of the stack ready to ambush him.

At home in his seminary apartment, Kurt raided the ancient Frigidaire for the last bottle of ginger ale. Thus fortified, he ripped open the letter.

He had failed three areas: pastoral care, ethics, and Church and culture.

For the first time, doubts flew at him like the winged

furies. No! He stood up, shouting at the cherry blossoms right outside his window. God Himself had given Kurt a vision of his call to the ordained ministry five years ago in a healing service, and he had never wavered in his confidence in God's will for his life.

Just then, he heard his wife, Debbie, fumbling for her keys outside the door. He knew she'd be laden with briefcase, diaper bag, and purse, trying to balance young, wiggly Kurt on her hip; yet he could not move to help her. Finally, she stumbled in, set baby Kurt down, and closed the door. Kurt toddled over to his daddy expecting a hug. As Debbie slid out of her raincoat, she said cautiously, "I guess you heard today."

"Dada!" screamed Kurt, his arms flung wide. "Dada up!"

Kurt ignored the baby and thrust the letter at Debbie. The baby started to cry. "Dada! Dada!"

Debbie read the letter while baby Kurt whimpered for his daddy. "I'm sorry," she said, and reached out to embrace him. "I guess God has different plans right now."

"No!" shouted Kurt, ignoring the baby now sobbing and clinging to his trousers. "No! God gave me the vision of being ordained, and nothing is going to stop me." He pushed the baby away. "Go away. Not now."

Howling, the baby ran to Debbie and burrowed in her skirt. She leaned down to comfort him.

"I will be ordained. I will. I'll get another bishop. I'll find another diocese. I'll do remedial work. I'm going to be a priest. It's all I've worked for for five years now. This is not going to stop me. You watch." Kurt crumpled the letter and hurled it across the room. The tight wad of paper smacked the lampshade, toppling Debbie's favorite porcelain lamp, which shattered on by hardwood floor.

Baby Kurt stopped crying and peeked out from his mother's skirt. His blotchy face looked in astonishment at his angry father. "Dada scary."

Debbie said quietly, "Maybe you better look at what you're worshiping here: your ordination, or Jesus."

❧

What does it mean to worship lesser gods? Baptized and confirmed Christians have publicly renounced all other gods but God. Unfortunately, accepting Christ doesn't give any of us a bubble of protection from the snares of the enemy. As humans, we are tempted in a variety of ways, but idolatry tempts us to put something other than God at the center of our lives. We live this out by devoting our best energies, the bulk of our time, and the crème de la crème of our imaginations to anything (people, ideas, or objects) other than the Lord.

This displacement of God is what I mean by "worshiping" lesser gods. Generally, Christians don't banish God to the periphery on purpose. It's just that other things creep in and take root, growing in importance as the space devoted to God shrinks in our hearts.

Worshiping other gods often catches us off guard, our lives slipping out of proportion before we know what's happened. How does it happen, for instance, that I come to love my job more than God? When does the need to control my children become more important than God's will for them? Why am I suddenly consumed with too much church work and not enough worship time? The enemy is sneaky and persistent and delights every time we give our best to anything other than God Himself. The heart of idolatry is really selfishness. We think we're going to get more out of our devotion to something else than our devotion to God. This misplaced loyalty is the lie of Satan, and we must learn to resist.

The temptation to go after the lesser prize instead of the greater is a subtle one. I am continually amazed and discouraged by my own readiness to let almost anything usurp God's place in the center of my being. Perhaps the reason is the all-too-human fear that God won't produce what we need after all. Perhaps we think God's silence equals God's impotence, or His indifference to our survival. As a result, we turn to something more palpable, more tangible—our own golden calf, comfortingly real in the face of a God the Israelites couldn't see or name.

For better or worse, our earthly experience of seeking truth in Christ doesn't feel like an organized hike on a well-marked trail. Instead, it is a journey of stumbling, backtracking, guessing, slipping, grumbling, hoping, and praying as God guides us with His vision for us (Ps. 32:8)—a vision we can barely make out through our cataracts of desire and need. Truly, here and now we see through a glass darkly; and in this world browned out by sin, reflective luminaries often look like the real thing. These lesser gods fool us, leading us into deception and lies, destroying harmony in our personal relations and in our spiritual journeys as well. Without knowing fully what we are doing, we hide the things we secretly love and admire under our skirts, like Rachel, sitting primly and righteously on our camels, wondering why we are not whole, why we still suffer, why we feel unreconciled to the God we profess. We think we've fooled God, when it's only ourselves we've deceived.

Several interesting truths emerge from Rachel's story. First, she didn't see any harm in taking the little statuettes. She might as well abscond with them; maybe they'd serve as a lucky talisman. Rachel didn't realize that even little "harmless" pet idols bring with them a price, and nobody escapes the consequences. The destruction may not be as dramatic as an atomic mushroom cloud, but our souls suffer in some way when we place anything between us and God. We lose precious warmth and intimacy, replacing trust in God with the hard, tight ball of fear. We reverse Pinocchio's evolution—we trade in our real lives to become puppets of masters who, like the greedy showmaster, do not love us.

Under the Old Covenant, God's punishments and rewards

were swift and unmistakable. Though the New Covenant emphasizes grace and offers Jesus as a mediator, we still suffer when we do not give all of ourselves to God. Living under the New Covenant gives us the opportunity to confess our sins and to give up our golden calves, our lesser gods. Then we become open to receive the blessings offered by a God who demands our total commitment but who rewards it by replacing our rinky-dink desires with something bigger and more perfect than we could ever achieve on our own.

The final word, then, is not despair over our condition but hope, joy, and redemption—always redemption! Because of the cross, we are freed from the trappings of idolatry. As Christians seeking Jesus, our eyes are opened more and more as we grope toward the light of God's truth in His Word. If we let Him, like a loving parent Jesus gently takes our faces, cupping His hand under our chins, and turns our sight away from the world's attractive lures, then refocuses our vision on Him.

This book explores how we are seduced by the lesser gods—sometimes in ignorance, sometimes in willfulness—and how Jesus frees us from bondage to anything, even good things, less satisfying or meaningful or fulfilling than Himself. It is a book of hope and of gratitude for Christ's gift of freedom from the natural human condition of sin and false desire.

It is also a book for those of us who don't have faith down perfectly yet, who can relate to the Israelites whining in the desert. I am not a theologian, and the only way I can look at the puzzle of idolatry is through experience. My problem is that though I may have grasped the dilemma and the solution intellectually, my emotions and spiritual life have been much slower to respond. I can't simply say, "Aha! So that's the problem!" and change myself overnight. I need an ocean of grace and years to swim through it.

My daily struggle against idolatry and other forms of sin can be summed up in a prayer given to Stockton and me by friends:

> Dear Lord,
>
> So far today, I've done all right. I haven't gossiped, haven't lost my temper, haven't been greedy, grumpy, nasty, selfish, or over-indulgent. I'm really glad about that.
>
> But in a few minutes, God, I'm going to get out of bed, and from then on I'm probably going to need a lot more help.
>
> Thank You, in Jesus' name, Amen.

The "harmless" lesser gods keep us in a wrong relation to God Almighty. Fortunately, God gives us His grace and "a lot more help" to overcome them.

Chapter 2

CHRISTIAN MINISTRY AND SERVICE

This is the work of God, that you believe in him.

—JOHN 6:29

Blade looked around the room at his friends in the Bible study group, struggling to answer the question at hand. "Because I was looking for meaning. Because I wanted to be helpful." Blade hitched his hand-sewn Italian leather shoe onto his opposite knee, shifting uncomfortably. "I went down to the Homeless Center in the first place because I thought I was called. By God. You know, my ministry." Picking at invisible filaments on his slacks, Blade tried to disguise his angst from the rest of the group. He sensed his muddy inner pool of emotions beginning to gurgle danger-ously, threatening to overflow. Why? Why? Why would a wealthy, well-traveled, thirty-five-year-old bachelor allow a group of bums to undo him, making him feel like weeping in front of his Bible study and ministry support group? Blade locked his arms tightly across his chest.

Pastor Johnson, a slightly deaf, older gentleman, whose appearance always reminded Blade of a sheaf of wheat, cleared his throat. He toyed with a pipe he hadn't lit in twenty years. "Ah, what do you think is the problem here?" he probed gently.

A sound tree cannot bear evil fruit, nor can a bad tree bear good fruit. . . . Thus you will know them by their fruits (Matt. 7:18, 20). Today's verse had ignited the whole issue for Blade, and he wished the pastor would move on to Mrs. Whitliff, who was bursting to brag about the proceeds of the church garage sale. He envied Mrs. Whitliff. Her ministry was clear-cut, defined, and seemed to arrive in her heart like a telegram from God Himself. She never had doubts about what the Lord wanted from her. Her inner pool of emotions never got murky with questions like his.

Blade eyed the other five members of the group. If there were a safe place to thrash out one's spiritual doubts, this cozy room in the pastor's home was it. "You remember last year when I sold the clothing company—I was set finan-cially for life, but I didn't want to be a leech on society. I wanted to help the community. Pastor Johnson suggested that I go downtown to the center for homeless men."

He continued, "One thing led to another. I wanted to teach them to help themselves instead of just feeding them, you know, so I started a woodworking program, making birdfeeders and letterholders and other wood-items like the stamp dispensers.

"At first, I felt exhilarated. The projects gave the men a feeling of worth, gave them something to do, and made money for them and the shelter. It was great." Blade paused, wondering how to phrase this next part without sounding like a stingy, selfish person. He didn't want the group to get the wrong idea about him.

"Then the men started stealing the tools and some of the scraps of wood. From the start I knew there was that possibility, but I felt disappointed anyway. Still, I didn't let that stop me. I bought new tools and more wood."

"My dear, you're a saint," interjected Mrs. Whitliff. "Don't you hate it when you're trying to be nice and people take advantage?"

"Go ahead," said the pastor, scratching his disheveled hair and twirling the bowl of his empty pipe.

"Well, I don't really know when it started happening, but I realized I had put several thousand dollars into this project and wasn't getting a dime in return. Some of the men disappeared, too. And last week this one guy got drunk and smashed five of the birdfeeders that were ready to sell."

Blade sighed. "The last straw came when I told Bob for the fiftieth time not to nail the ledge on backward; it upsets the balance, and the feeders won't stay upright. These men pay no attention to me. I don't know why I thought I could make a difference."

There. He'd almost said it all. The group looked at him sympathetically. Lindsey, next to him, patted the back of his jacket. "It's not easy, is it?" she affirmed.

Blundering on, he decided to finish. "Now the problem is that we've been working toward the St. Matthias' Craft Fair, and yesterday a TV news crew came out to do some publicity."

"What's the problem with that?" asked Mrs. Whitliff.

"The problem is that if we're going to have a decent showing—now that these stupid birdfeeders have become a public event—I'm going to have to spend eighteen hours a day down there getting ready for the fair. The men have slacked off, and I've had to cancel my trip to the Caymans just so the shelter won't look bad."

Blade finished picking at his slacks and uncrossed his arms. "You see, I was ready to quit and now I feel trapped. Worse than that, I feel like a failure. The men don't really care anymore, even with the fair. I see the whole thing clearly for the first time. What's really happened here is that I've used these men to feel good about myself."

Blade had lost all sense of what God had called him to

do. He was afraid that he no longer understood the whole idea of ministry.

WHAT IS MINISTRY?

What is ministry, anyway? In a metaphorical sense, ministry is what we all do when we pitch in to help with the great festival of God on earth. The church in its many aspects is like an ongoing feast or celebration; the tasks involved are many and varied, and pulling off an affair on such a grand scale makes good use of different gifts and talents, sprinkled generously among the helpers. From advertisement of the event, to serving food to the guests, to giving rides to the party, to providing a place to celebrate, to cooking, to cleaning, to organizing, to overseeing—cooperation is required for the great festival to continue.

Ministry is not sitting back and letting the ordained people do all the work.

New Testament connotations of ministry include the concept of work done in the name of Christ. The New Testament also mentions the ideas of service and mission as connected with ministry. Formal definitions of the word "ministry" connote caring for, helping, or attending to others' needs and wants. The picture we develop as we approach the heart of ministry is that of someone who (1) loves Christ, (2) shares the good news with others, (3) works unselfishly.

Over the centuries, we have made ministry more complex than it really is.

Blade's story highlights several snags in the process of discerning and carrying out the service we feel called to do for God. Our ministries these days are a complicated network of needs and callings and echoes of what we feel we should do, all fighting against what we'd like to do. On the one hand, if our hands are God's hands and our feet are God's feet in the world, then we are essential as workers in God's kingdom on earth. And yet what happens when we feel trapped, resentful? What ever happened to God, "whose service is perfect freedom?"[1]

A major problem occurs for me in ministry every time I shift my focus from God to the task at hand. When the ministry or the service itself becomes central, instead of God (like Blade when he became consumed with the birdfeeders and the craft fair and the publicity), then I begin to feel inadequate, or restless, or resentful, or frantic, or territorial. In other words, I begin to suffer from idolatry. I spend more time, energy, and effort working for God than listening to Him in prayer.

I started to examine the idea of "calling" last fall, after allowing myself to be coerced into taking charge of the kitchen for our church's annual tea, the proceeds of which go to community outreach. I had mistakenly thought the job was about food instead of about coordination on a massive scale. Being kitchen manager involved getting four thousand sandwiches, breads, desserts, and other goodies baked by volunteers, delivered to the church, sorted on silver trays, and served to hundreds of ladies chatting pleasantly around tables loaded with fine china and elegant centerpieces.

I nearly had a nervous breakdown before it was over.

"Why did You ever let me say 'yes'?" I whined to Jesus in my prayer time.

His answer: "So you would remember that tasks like that belong to someone else. You are not gifted in committee work."

"Oh," I said. "I'm sorry."

Accepting the job in the first place was Problem #1. I wasn't listening in my prayer time. Once I had accepted the job, Problem #2 was that I focused on the impossibility of dealing with four thousand delectable but perishable items. I should never, not for one minute, have taken my eyes off the sight of Jesus, who was undoubtedly shaking His head at me bumbling around in an apron smeared with flour dust.

Problem #3 was my unwillingness to relinquish the mental image I had of being a clergy wife capable of running the kitchen for the Episcopal Church Women's largest annual fundraiser. My pride got in the way. I worshiped this image I had of myself more than I worshiped God. If I had listened well and prayed for guidance before making the decision, I would have heard God saying, "I don't think so. I have other plans for you. Somebody else is much better equipped for this job, and if you take it, you will deny this other person the opportunity to shine for My glory."

But no. I barged in and took the job.

The German philosopher Georg Wilhelm Friedrich Hegel, 1770–1831, proposed a way of looking at all religion—in fact, all of life—in terms of dialectic, a tension between two polar opposites, thesis and antithesis. Any two paradoxical truths, he said, need to be resolved in a synthesis, bringing together two seemingly opposing things in a new and creative way. The pushes and pulls we feel as we try to discern God's work for us can be examined in Hegelian terms as a series of opposites we need to bring together through prayer: our needs versus others' needs; ordinary service versus special service; God's success versus worldly success; faith versus works. These are sets of contrasts that bear closer examination.

OUR NEEDS VERSUS OTHERS' NEEDS

Ideally, what we do for God should not only benefit the people we are serving, but should also satisfy our own deepest needs as well. Like comfortable shoes, our service should "fit" us as we walk through our Christian journeys. However, sometimes we find ourselves miserable in our Christian service, lame from shoes filled with tacks and pebbles.

One of our choir's favorite anthems is a lilting piece entitled "Here I Am," a hymn that evokes our worthiest, purest desire to serve the One calling in the night. Most of us in the choir can't warble our way through the lyrics without tears in our eyes, recalling the amazing fact that God does call us and does use whatever we give Him.

So what happens between our sanctified desire to serve God and the anger we feel at old men who steal tools and smash birdfeeders? On the one hand we seem to burst at the seams with the need to be useful, to be needed, to share our gifts with people. On the other hand, the people we serve also have needs, some more complex and bewildering, and certainly—we find—more demanding and less holy, than our own. Our ministries crumble and die because we cannot resolve the tension between two sets of needs.

The group of men and women who gathered at my husband's ten-year seminary reunion had matured and seasoned considerably compared to the crowd of eager, starry-eyed young priests who had sprung forth from the seminary ten years earlier. Several had switched to secular careers. Several had already returned to the seminary for the six-week burn-out course. One had renounced his vows. Not a single person had escaped the inevitable confrontation between personal needs and expectations and others' needs and expectations.

This collision is no less real for those of us in lay ministries. Working with the homeless is a noble involvement, but, just like anybody else, sometimes they smell bad, sometimes they're rude, many times they are mentally ill, alcoholic, emotionally disturbed. They do not curtsy on the other side of the food line or thank us for being there to serve them.

Volunteering at the hospital introduces us to people who throw up on our shoes, or die before we can get the real chaplain, or simply turn their faces to the wall because they cannot hear the message of hope we thought we could bring to them.

And when we volunteered to teach Sunday school, we didn't count on the utter stubbornness of the co-teacher who insisted on using the (terrible) curriculum she developed over the summer. Nor were we prepared for the smart mouths from the eighth grade girls who finally reduced us to tears, alone in the bathroom after class.

Even if we know the downside as we go into a new ministry, we are still, often, beaten by the graphic realities of the service we undertake in God's name. At some level, we expect to be fed in spite of the difficulties. So how do we synthesize our needs and the demands of the job? How do we know whether to hang in there and learn from our circumstances or quit and find something more rewarding? Despite the odds, a large number of Stockton's seminary classmates had stuck with the job, and had begun to unearth hidden challenges and even rewards. How did they get over the hump? How did they find the strength to keep digging?

Every position is different, of course, but the common theme throughout all our questions over ministry is prayer, prayer, prayer. Mother Teresa strikes me as the classic contemporary example of someone who synthesized her own deepest spiritual needs with others' deepest needs. Yet how did she stand the death, the scabs, the filth, the germs, the smells day in and day out? In a book entitled *Mother Teresa: A Simple Path*, she revealed how others could follow her simple path: "All we, or anyone else, needed to do was to pray and start loving one another more."[2]

Prayer and love. How simple. How impossible without God.

In true God-given ministry, we become so absorbed in God's will that our own needs seem to evaporate. Here is the key for Mother Teresa: "This kind of service . . . isn't about doing for the poor, but about being there in their suffering, sharing it with Christ."[3] Doing something for someone fences us outside their experience, distancing us as the "other" in their lives. True ministry of any real nature involves our becoming one in spirit with those we are called to serve.

No wonder Christian ministry is more difficult than social work. No wonder it is ultimately more rewarding.

The more we are willing to identify with the people we help, the more Christ ignites the relationship—and the more our needs and the needs of others meld into one, all served, as it turns out, by Christ.

By the same token, it's no surprise that we suffer in our ministries. However, this suffering can be either self-centered or other-centered. On the one hand, we suffer, whining because the job is more burdensome or bothersome than we thought, and besides, we aren't getting any pleasure out of it. On the other hand, we suffer through identification with the pain of others. Back to the opening example: If Blade's pastor is wise, he will tell him, "Of course it's difficult. Pray, Blade, pray relentlessly until you feel in tune with what Christ wants from you. Expect pain. Expect inconvenience. Otherwise, you might as well forget it and move permanently to the Caymans."

Blade is moving in the right direction. Because he is able to discern his own neediness in feeling good about himself as a Christian, he is now ready for the next step: to give up his self-image as a good guy "saving" the poor. By doing this, he can move into an ultimately more rewarding stage: he can put aside his needs and enter more fully into the lives of the men—if he discerns that working with the homeless is indeed what God wants him to do.

The biblical image for ministry referred to in *A Simple Path* is not of Christ's followers bustling about doing good but of Mary and St. John at the foot of the cross with Jesus. This image stands over and against other stories of serving, such as Peter's mother-in-law, who cooked dinner after Jesus healed her. Or the story of Martha. It must have been easier for Martha or Peter's mother-in-law to serve Jesus supper than it was for John simply to stay with Jesus as He died. Both actions are ministry, and both are helpful. Yet John entered into a new dimension of being, of oneness with Christ's suffering, while Martha focused on her own needs, becoming resentful when she felt her sister wasn't doing her share.

When we become one with those we serve, willing to participate in their suffering, we quit worrying about whether our needs are being met or not.

The recovery movement and twelve-step programs have done much for healing broken or undefined selves, crippled from painful pasts. I have been grateful for support groups that have helped me to differentiate my self from unhealthy demands placed on me by other, more abusive or manipulative selves. If we do not distinguish our selves from others, we risk becoming the designated pack horse in an unhealthy family or church system. We are then not free to choose or discern the service Christ has picked especially for us. We allow ourselves to be loaded up like donkeys with others' agendas. Boundaries are essential; the self must be independent and free to choose service to Christ, not stuck with servitude. As my friend Vicky Shaw says, "Otherwise, we become slaves, not servants"—the difference is essential.

A word of caution, however. If we get bogged down in the stage of self-differentiation, we are also not free to choose. We remain aloof, apart, separate, and unwilling to sacrifice for other people. We do not enter into the flow of humanity. The synthesis between others' needs and our needs is to develop and maintain a healthy sense of who we are and what God wants us to do. We need to be able to say both "no" and "yes" to service.

A corollary to the discussion of needs is the obvious and spectacular fact that God embellishes each ordinary life with unique skills and talents. As responsible Christians, we need to take an honest inventory of the special gifts God has given us (no false modesty here) and seek situations in which these gifts shine to God's glory. A cursory glance at my life shows that I am an ignoramus at math, but I am a good cook. Therefore, a bad use of my talents would be to volunteer as the church treasurer. A better use of my time is some sort of culinary ministry. As a result, I have felt called to serve on the consolation committee for funeral receptions. I don't have to organize the event (thank goodness), but I gain great satisfaction from preparing casseroles, slicing strawberries, making dip, serving iced tea for people during a time of mourning. Granted, the schedule is often hectic or inconvenient—recently our parish had four deaths in one week—nevertheless, I feel deeply centered in Christ through this service.

Another way God connects our hearts with those we serve is through the "give-back effect." During the last few years when so many of my family members died, funeral receptions honoring my loved ones in cities far away touched me at a vulnerable time. Watching women I didn't know tenderly prepare cookies, sandwiches, delicacies in panoramic spreads of color helped me understand the communal nature of grief. I wanted to be a part of the age-old women's business of helping with the dead. God used my experience so that I could enter into and help alleviate the pain of others' experiences.

Questions to ask when floundering about in the issues of ministry include, What am I passionate about? What am I good at? In what activities do I lose myself? What allows for God's glory, not mine? God uses us best in those ways that quicken our hearts, springing on us opportunities to make holy our gifts and experience. After the small group meeting related at the beginning of the story, Pastor Johnson finally asked Blade what he loved to do most. Blade said sheepishly, "Well, I loved being a business executive. I was very good at it." Together Blade and the pastor prayed for discernment for the best use of Blade's gifts. Several phone calls and a month later, Blade was installed as the new director of the homeless shelter. The previous director had hated the business end of the job and had almost led the organization into bankruptcy. As director, Blade's most obvious gifts were utilized—and he was also able to deal directly with the men on a personal basis. He told the pastor, "I've never felt so fulfilled."

ORDINARY SERVICE VERSUS SPECIAL SERVICE

Sometimes the happy circumstance of having our needs met goes overboard. Our special ministry becomes an ego trip and an excuse not to tend to those around us day to day. A friend relates her experiences growing up: "My parents became converted to Christianity, and after that I never saw them on the weekends. They volunteered for every Cursillo team, every Faith Alive, every available retreat in a six-state area. They lived for these events. But they forgot about us.

"One weekend, my grandmother was staying with us. The washing machine broke, the cat fractured her hip, the car had a flat tire, and Gramma couldn't get me to my soccer finals in Dallas. I missed out on the championship game. My parents came home on a religious high, clearly bored with mundane stuff like a broken dishwasher or missing a soccer game.

"I stopped going to church after that. I wasn't interested in a God who had stolen my parents away."

In contrast, I know another woman who is an ordained Lutheran minister. After she'd had two children, I ran into her at a wedding and asked her how her ministry was going. "Oh, I've quit my job at the church. My children are my ministry now."

What blessed children!—to have a mom willing to sacrifice the rewards of preaching, teaching, counseling, celebrating the Eucharist so that she could devote her Christian service to raising children.

What a blessed woman, too, to be in a financial position to offer her skills and talents to her children during those early, formative years. Yet even if she'd been forced by circumstances—or chosen—to work outside the home, having the attitude that her children are her ministry gives them dignity and priority.

This woman had obviously prayed about how God wanted her to use her gifts, and she selected the more "ordinary" service for Christ—making peanut butter sandwiches, running a taxi service, arbitrating emotional disputes over who gets the bigger cookie. Though she recognized the importance of doing God's work in the church—and planned to go back to the ordained ministry when her children were older—she also valued the mundane, ordinary ways we serve Christ in those we live with. All ministry is Christ's ministry, in and through us, lay or ordained.

Or take my husband. As an ordained minister of a large parish, one of his "ministries" is attending various parties given by our parishioners. However, as a member of our household, one of his "ministries" at home is yard work. Guess which ministry he prefers? Guess which ministry fulfills more of his needs? Because my husband strives to be faithful to Christ in all respects, he spends Friday morning mowing, raking, and bagging leaves—and other parts of the weekend celebrating with his parishioners. For him, the ordinary services like bagging leaves are just as important as the more exciting ministries like weddings and receptions and christening parties.

A third friend spent his teenage years alone while his

father traveled around the country speaking to large religious groups. My friend recalls the madcap drives to the airport (his father always ran late), the phone calls disrupting dinner, the glow in his father's eyes when he related the glamour of the trip. "No question," says my friend, "my dad saved a lot of people around the country. Now, years later, Dad loves to talk about all the bigwigs he knows. The sad thing is, I'm not sure he could even tell you how old we are."

My friend's father certainly didn't have the problem of not having his needs met by his ministry. In fact, he'd become inflated with self-importance through the adulation of the crowds he spoke to. My friend's father had chosen a "special" ministry over an "ordinary" one and had essentially abandoned his children in order to save the world.

Human nature being what it is, I know I'm more likely to be enticed by a ministry that excites me, not day-in and day-out annoying, exhausting chores. I'd much rather teach adult Sunday school than do laundry, for example. At the same time, my family needs clean clothes. I'm working on my attitude. If I can think of laundry as a ministry, if I can visualize Christ smiling and holding the fresh, hot towels, then all the sorting, washing, drying, and folding becomes a sacred task instead of a grinding chore.

So far, the examples I've used have been mostly parent-child relationships, but the principle of ordinary ministry works for everyone. We all live in some kind of community, and the very dailiness of the contact with others can lead to monotony. Instead, if we view crotchety Aunt Matilda or querulous Joe in the office next door as Jesus Himself, then every human touch, every comment, every judgment, every gesture we make as we move through our ordinary days becomes a ministry.

The synthesis of ordinary ministry and the special ministries we are called to from time to time is that, ultimately, every breath we take in all circumstances—whether washing out a bedpan for a dying parent or speaking before twenty-five thousand people—is service for Christ. We do not have to give up the special ministries for the ordinary ones, or vice versa. If we are in the necessarily continual process of prayerful discernment, then we are ready for anything. Our lives become our ministries.

GOD'S SUCCESS VERSUS WORLDLY SUCCESS

My friend whose father was a public speaker used to rationalize his father's absence, saying, "How can I compare the thousands upon thousands of lives touched by my dad's speeches with the measly handful of family left at home? It's selfish for three people to demand his time over the vast ministry he has."

As an adult, my friend has changed his mind. Though the American mindset of "more is better" makes it difficult to argue against the success of sheer numbers, my friend has concluded, "Actually, I don't think the final judgment has much to do with numbers at all."

Correct. The success of any given ministry isn't measured in worldly terms. Human response according to our yardsticks of dollars or numbers or fan letters simply doesn't apply. The determiner of our ministry's success is our obedience to the call of God, even if it means, like Jeremiah, that people hate us and throw us into the well. Jeremiah was hardly successful in the world's terms, but in God's terms, he's at the top of the chart—he was obedient in the face of disaster.

Look at the "success" of Jesus' ministry. He did not consider Himself a bigshot. Yes, He mesmerized large crowds, but He also humbled Himself as a footwasher to His friends. The week before Easter, His ministry peaked in terms of popularity. Hundreds of people shouted, "Hosanna!", threw palm branches under His feet, and wanted to make Him king. One week later, His fans had been reduced to one who betrayed Him, one who denied Him, nine who disappeared, a cluster of women who watched from afar (according to Matthew, Mark, and Luke), and one disciple (according to John) who stayed with Him, along with His mother and a few friends, as He died. How can a ministry that ends in ignominious death with only one devotee and a parent left be considered successful in anyone's terms?

And yet.

A minister we know has left a stable and successful pastorship to start a new church outside a large metropolitan area. Most people think he's crazy. He'll be penniless for at least a year, and he plans to traipse the streets and cul-de-sacs of suburbia, ringing strangers' doorbells and using other evangelistic techniques to connect people with Jesus Christ. My hat goes off to this man and his family. He feels called by God, and he's responding in the face of disbelief and incredulity. Whether his church makes it or not is not the point—God will tend to the results. The important thing is that he has obeyed his personal call for service.

For me the watershed of this issue came in my call to write. The symbol for my struggle was a terra-cotta Christus Rex hanging on the wall across from the couch where I prayed, a primitive flat clay symbol of the resurrection. From across the room, the Christ had no mouth. On closer examination, one could feel with fingertips a raised circle, an "O" of a mouth, unpainted, almost invisible.

Was Christ speaking to me or not? Was I called to speak for Him or not? What I couldn't reconcile was almost twenty years of rejection slips with an unquenchable fire of a call to write. If God wanted me to write, why did so many doors slam in my face? For many years, I tried to sell various ideas and manuscripts. I'd run off twenty-five copies of a book proposal, write twenty-five nice letters, bundle each into a manilla envelope, and send them off to publishers. Then, I'd sit back and wait for the mail.

One by one (and some days, three or four at a time), I'd receive my queries back in the mailbox. "We're sorry. We don't want your book."

I literally have notebooks filled with all kinds of rejection letters: polite, abrupt, encouraging, rude, standardized. Over the years, I tried various ways of dealing with the dilemma. I tried to stop writing, to ignore Christ's demand, to pretend that writing was my own desire and not a call from a higher authority. I'd even gone back to school to get a Ph.D. to avoid the pain of this unreconciled call. In my lowest moments, I even wondered if I'd been tricked by the adversary into believing that Jesus wanted me to do something that so obviously wasn't working out.

My spiritual advisor helped me greatly. Eventually, I came to see that the call was real, and if the only two people who ever read what I wrote were my my husband and my mother, then I had to continue regardless of the rejection. I was not writing so that a publishing company would make good on the deal. I was writing to Christ, for Christ, and Him alone. Wanting to be published was, for me, idolatry.

The most disturbing Bible story in connection with a "failed" ministry is that of Cain and Abel. Cain's ministry failed before God. God rejected the offering of fruits and grain, the symbol of Cain's service. How deeply that rejection must have wounded Cain—and then to see the Lord accept Abel's offering with approval. The Bible doesn't tell us exactly why God rejected Cain's offering (possibly because it wasn't the first fruits), but it is clear that Cain's response is not the correct one. The lesson in this story is not to smite anyone else in a jealous rage; rather, for me, it was to look deeper into my own heart and purify the offering; to get rid of my selfishness; to disinvest my plans, my hopes, my dreams for the outcome.

Success or lack of success belongs to God. To serve means to obey in spite of worldly results. Sometimes God's success matches worldly success. Sometimes God's success cannot be measured with any earthly barometer. The fact remains: Worrying about measurable success is worshiping the wrong god.

FAITH VERSUS WORKS

The medieval church had the faith versus works dilemma licked. Penitents paid for every sin they committed by saying rosaries and Hail Marys, and faithful church members bought time out of purgatory by doing other good works such as buying splintery pieces of the "true cross" or giving to the poor. The formula was simple: The more works you performed, the more rewards you got in heaven.

Then Martin Luther came along in the mid-sixteenth century and bashed the system with his focus on salvation by grace. He threw the tidy faith/works package away, forcing people to reexamine the relationship between what we believe and how our service reflects those beliefs.

The Bible itself presents a polarity between what is important for Christians. In Acts 16:31 Paul and Silas answer the question, "What must I do to be saved?" by responding, "Believe in the Lord Jesus." In other words, faith is all you need—you cannot earn salvation by doing something to win God's favor. This is one part of the equation, but not the whole story. To counter those who believe but are content to do nothing except sit on their behinds instead of acting out their faith, James reminds his audience that "For as the body apart from the spirit is dead, so faith apart from works is dead" (2:26). Even the Bible presents us with a dialectic between faith and works.

My favorite Gospel story used to illustrate the faith/works predicament is Luke 10:38–42, the story of Mary and Martha. This story works in conjunction with another Mary and Martha story, John 12:1–8. In both stories, Martha is serving Jesus by preparing Him a meal, while Mary is either sitting at His feet listening to Him or anointing His feet with expensive spikenard. In both stories, Jesus affirms Mary. In Luke, He counters Martha's complaint by saying that Mary has made the right choice to sit and listen to Him; in John, He counters Judas's accusation that the oil is a waste of money better spent on the poor: "Let her alone. . . . The poor you always have with you, but you do not always have me" (John 12:7–8).

The point is clear. Serving Christ takes a backseat to worshiping Him.

38

If this injunction is true, and if Martin Luther is right, then why are we concerned about our works at all? Why is there a gap between our faith and our works? If we listen to Jesus, our faith will determine what we do for Him. Mary wasn't concerned with doing for Christ; her actions flowed naturally out of her worship of Him. Her service was not just an expression of her faith, it *was* her faith. Works and faith merged as she anointed His feet.

Several assumptions lurk within the twentieth-century American religious climate, undermining our attempts to bring together our faith and our works. First is the American myth of independence, the old bootstraps philosophy. In spite of the biblical teaching that we are saved by grace alone, we still believe that our salvation in some way depends on what we do and how well we do it. The snake still weasles in, tempting us to believe that our service to Christ makes a difference to our salvation. We feel the pangs, the throbbing, the desire to win God's approval by our actions.

We argue that worship alone isn't enough. Faith alone isn't enough. We need to prove to God that we care. And doesn't the Bible also say we need to help others? Feed the poor? Take care of the widows?

Yes, of course. The problem comes when we allow our worship to become separate from our service, when we "take on" tasks because we feel we have to.

The flawed theology also hides out in clever epigrams

like, "Who you are is God's gift to you. What you make of yourself is your gift to God." This saying is not heretical; it simply isn't accurate. Who I am is God's gift to me, yes. However, what I make of myself is also God's gift to me. God has given me the education, the opportunities, the encouragement, the discipline to become who I am. Everything is a gift. I must make the decision to follow Jesus Christ, but after that, my service to God is really one more gift He gives me.

Our works are a direct result of the meshing of faith and God's grace, merging in prayer. Ideally, our whole life blossoms in a continual prayer—our works, our worship, every element of our existence is offered to God through prayer as our service. Benedictine monks traditionally make no distinction between faith and work. They call prayer opus dei, the work of the Lord.

TO STAND AND WAIT

Prayer, then, seems to be the mediator as competing forces play tug of war with the different aspects of Christian service. Our needs and others' needs meet, and Christ serves both when we listen to what He wants us to do. Taking our cue from Jesus' life of ministry, we see that He handled a large public ministry without sacrificing or neglecting to serve those closest to Him on a daily basis. Again using our Lord as an example, we see clearly that the success or failure of any ministry is relative and cannot be measured in worldly terms. Obedience constitutes successful ministry. And finally, the distinction between faith and works disappears as service flows naturally out of prayer.

A wise priest once told me that it didn't really matter what we do for Christ. Consumed at the time with a particular ministry I felt called to, I listened politely, but inside I disagreed. Of course it mattered what you did! What you did was the whole crux of faith!

Now that I am older and (presumably) wiser, I see the truth in his words. What we do for Jesus is vastly less important than who we are in Him. The crucial thing is to show up for duty daily, letting Him guide us into the ministry He needs accomplished—not the ministry we are on fire to accomplish on His behalf.

Letting go of the certainty of our calling and the self-gratification of our gifts is one of the first steps toward true service. Ironically, often the crushing shame of the failure of our own plans is the starting point of a ministry in humility.

The Puritan English writer John Milton offers a final insight into the meaning of true service for Christ. A great poet and Puritan writer during the English Civil War, Milton went blind in 1652. Though he later continued his political activities and went on to write the great classic *Paradise Lost*, Milton despaired when he first lost his sight. In his sonnet "When I Consider How My Light Is Spent," he expresses his fear that God's gift of words will be lodged useless in his dark sockets, while at the same time, his soul is bent with a greater desire to serve God.

In the poem, a voice named "Patience" answers his dilemma, saying that God doesn't need our work or our gifts. Those serve Him best who simply bear His yoke. The famous last line of the sonnet concludes, "They also serve who only stand and wait."[4]

God eventually showed Milton how he could serve Him through his words, but we are wise to take note of Milton's momentary paralysis. We serve God also when we stand in the darkness waiting and listening for His Word.

Christ is the foundation, not only for our service, but also for our total being. He is the real security for every aspect of our lives.

Chapter 3

SECURITY

He said to his disciples, "Therefore I tell you, do not be anxious about your life."

—LUKE 12:22

In the fifties, when I grew up, many of our friends had bomb shelters in their backyards. Most were spherical concrete bubbles partially submerged, with a door at ground level and steps inside leading down to a round, subterranean room. Inside, canned goods, blankets, drinking water, radios, lanterns, books, and other necessities of life crowded the shelves. Pipes leading to the outside allowed ventilation. Theoretically, these bomb shelters provided security in case of a nuclear attack.

As an adult, having seen pictures of the damage done by Little Boy and Fat Man to the Japanese cities of Hiroshima and Nagasaki, the idea that a tiny bomb shelter could protect us from a direct hit seems unbelievable, almost laughable. Even if we'd been spared a direct hit, judging from what we know about radiation, the ventilation systems would probably have piped in contaminated air, resulting in slow, miserable deaths for those inside the shelters. Though these bunkers might have afforded security against traditional bomber raids, in retrospect, they were little defense against the raging destruction of an atomic bomb.

Whether they provided real safety or not, the shelters did provide a feeling of security. Families could rest assured they had done everything possible to avoid uninvited disaster from the enemy.

As humans, we seem to need security in many forms— financial security, security in our own skins, security of position, security of place, safety from harm, none of which is provided by the world. Psalm 4 says, "for only you, Lord, make me dwell in safety."[1] We should all sleep like babies every night knowing we are children of the Lord, yet we look to stock portfolios, popularity, jobs, social standing, and other things to give us the security only God can give. We continually construct little emotional bomb shelters, ignoring the more profound gift God offers us, the deep sense that things are all right within us, that in Him we are safe at home.

Trusting in any of our homemade illusions of security instead of the true security of God is idolatry. But, oh, how subtly this one tempts us! If we are realistic at all and read the papers, we see clearly how fragile life is, how fragile we are. We need fortresses against disaster, pain, and loss. We forget that God became a human being with bones that break as easily as ours, with feelings as woundable as ours, and with emotional and physical needs like food, clothes, habitation, friends, and even a town to claim as home.

If God knows our needs before we ask Him, then why is it easier to depend on physical evidence to give us security? How can we claim the promise that our Heavenly Father will clothe us like the lilies of the field? How can we count on the fact that He's numbered the hairs on our heads and will keep us safe from harm?

SECURITY OF PLACE

As Christians, we are citizens of a country that can't be found on a map. Spiritually, we are aliens on the earth. Our home, heaven, is in another dimension altogether, and no matter where we live, the earth will always be a slightly foreign place.

However, while we live here on earth, place matters. Even Jesus was labeled "Jesus of Nazareth." Of Nazareth. Jesus was not just from the country of Israel or the region of the Middle East. He was from a particular town, and from a particular family in that town. His lineage was important; and Matthew takes great pains to place Jesus as the descendant of Abraham and David. Though God is universal, Jesus was a specific man from a specific place with a specific family.

We, too, are specific individuals, and the particulars of our lives are important because they define us and shape us. There is no such thing as a generic American Christian. Where we're from becomes part of who we are. (Just ask any native Texan whether Texas is special or not. The identity of "Texan" goes deep, though El Paso is as different from Tyler as any two cities can be.) Having lived as an adult both in Texas and in the Washington, D.C., area, I've noticed that the expression of faith is realized differently in the Bible Belt than in the East. For one example, kids' Sunday morning soccer games are taken for granted in the East, while they are the exception in the Bible Belt because so many people are in church.

Planted here for a short stint in these fleshly bodies, we long for a cozy spot on the earth, where people recognize us in the hardware store and can remember the time we hit the homerun and broke Mr. Magruder's plate glass window, where we can eat chicken fried steak (or crawfish, or lobster, or collard greens) with our buddies and laugh and talk deep into the night. Yet a tension operates in this issue. While we long for the safety of a hometown, at the same time, we want a place that doesn't trap us into a family stereotype.

Whether we like it or not, America in the nineties doesn't often allow us either the luxury or the stagnation of a hometown. The tradition of our country's strength is not in its roots, but in its mobility, its opportunities represented by flux, change, uprooting. I have lived in the following cities of Texas: Corpus Christi, Tyler, Kerrville, Leakey, Austin, Port Aransas, Dallas, San Antonio, Waco, Austin, Houston, and now Midland. The closest I can claim as "home" is to say I'm from Texas, although my family's roots are in Oklahoma, and as a child I also lived in Indiana and Connecticut.

For some people born and raised in the same town, the itinerary of those who move around may seem like an enviable adventure. They may feel suffocated by familiarity. The problem of security of place may not be a problem for some people, but for those of us shuttled from town to town growing up, the need to find a "home" on earth has implications for our spiritual lives. Until we can work through the need for security of place, we cannot fully embrace the good news that our home in heaven will not be another pit stop—that in Christ we can truly find the security for which we are looking elsewhere.

The need for security of place for me will always be represented by a new lunchroom at a new school. When we moved in the fifth grade, blessedly, all the students went home for lunch. When we moved in the seventh grade, I was not so lucky. My first day, I had to make it through the gauntlet of an unfamiliar lunch line. (Where were the trays, the silverware, the napkins? Which side was the correct line? Would I have enough money to get what I wanted? Where did I get a lunch ticket?) Then the real terrors began. I emerged from the line, tray in hand, looking out over a vast room of young adolescents. They were already bunched into cliques, seated at the long rows of tables laughing and talking. My stomach tightened, and I spotted an empty chair next to a girl in the green striped dress I recognized from one of my classes. I didn't care if she remembered me or not. She looked like a haven in the storm. I sat down. She continued talking with her friends. Silently I ate my lunch, grateful she let me sit beside her.

When we moved in the eighth grade, fortunately, the lunchroom was smaller, and I had managed to make a friend in the class right before lunch. After we moved in the ninth grade, the lunchroom once again became a dangerous place. I remember making it through the line that first day, standing with my tray, quietly desperate to find another outcast to join. The new lunchroom the next year wasn't quite as bad because I recognized some familiar faces from junior high, though my stomach tightened until I was safely seated between two people I knew.

I did not enjoy moving around.

However, because God redeems all our pain in one way or another, I learned some very valuable skills, such as how to make conversation with anyone, anywhere, and how to

learn names quickly. I also managed to salvage a few friend-
ships from the rush of moving in and out so quickly. In
fact, I married a friend from that dreadful ninth-grade year,
a handsome boy in my World Geography class, Stockton
Williams. In this case, the redemption has been far greater
than the pain.

The scars from an insecure background can mark our
spiritual development in several ways. First, the desire to
find a place of safety competes with the desire for God to
direct our lives. When we are desperate for the security
familiarity brings, we are tempted to ignore the nudgings
of God for us to move to a place He has prepared for us.
Perhaps people snug and happy in a safe hometown also
face the temptation to resist God's calling into the unknown.
Why leave what they know and love? Why rock the boat?

We are spiritual inheritors of the Semitic tradition, and
Semitic peoples wandered around a great deal. The Bible
is full of such wanderings. In fact, Jesus did not stay put in
Nazareth. He "wandered" where God led Him. Jesus also
sent out the twelve, two by two, into cities and villages to
preach and heal; and Paul and the early apostles traveled
all over the Roman Empire.

Some of us are called to stay in one place and witness
where we are. However, others are nudged and pulled to
places outside their comfort zones. The call of God becomes a threat to our safety if we've confused the security
of our community with the security of Jesus. Amazingly,

though, when we move out in obedience to Christ into the unfamiliar, we find ourselves closer to our real home than if we'd never taken that step of faith.

When Stockton gave up his secure job as a lawyer to go to seminary and we moved from our honeymoon home nestled among live oaks in Austin, I told Stockton, "I'll give up a big house and financial security and a swimming pool, but I'm not giving up my dream for a place by the river." Throughout my rocky teenage years, I had returned summer after summer to the Texas hill country, with its smell of juniper, fresh grass, and cypress-lined rivers. In my adult life, a place by the river in the Texas hill country symbolized stability for me. Every time we moved, my heart kindled anew for a place by the river. I dreamed at night about that place. I fantasized about the safe, warm feeling a place on the river would finally bring me.

After Stockton and I had trekked around the state serving various different churches, I finally realized that my yearning for the place on the river was really a yearning for God. The Texas hill country—though a beautiful and special place—is really just another dot on the map. The desire for home goes much deeper, and God calls us to Him through our longing for a secure place here on earth. We can tramp all over the world searching for a place to call home; and yet all along, we carry home inside us, accessible at all times through prayer. Though someday I still may build a cottage by the river, I see this desire now as an earthly house made of native stone and a tin roof, not a substitute for the security and bliss of heaven.

Our move to Midland was my thirty-second move. I am forty-five years old. What I finally learned—yes, I am a slow learner—is that my home is in Christ.

FINANCIAL SECURITY

Another way we seek false security instead of the security provided by the love of God is through dependence on money. At least one-third of Jesus' sayings have to do with money, and it is no accident that Timothy describes the love of money as the root of all evils (1 Tim. 6:10). The love of money reminds me of the secret treasure house in *The Jungle Book:* concealed deep in the jungle, vault-like decrepit ruins glow with the lure of rubies, diamonds, emeralds, crowns and necklaces of gold, strings of pearls . . . and snakes. Treasure seekers are drawn to the jewels; and when, bug-eyed, they can't let go their fists full of booty, the giant snakes bite and drown them, and they die still clutching their pearls. This metaphor works for all our misplaced love of money. When we place our security in cash, or bonds, or any form of material wealth instead of God, we are inevitably bitten in one way or another.

Money itself is not the evil. Our trust and love of it is the problem.

Literature provides a wealth of examples showing how the

wrong attitude toward money makes us miserable, in spite of our illusions that we think it will make us happy and secure. Consider, for example, nineteenth-century British writer George Eliot's *Silas Marner,* the classic tenth grade required reading. A lonely old miser, Silas hoards gold coins under his floorboards. An embittered handloom weaver, he is accused of a theft he didn't commit and leads a tragic life in the town of Raveloe. One night, all his money is stolen; but the same night, he takes in an unclaimed, yellow-haired baby girl. As the story evolves, Silas is redeemed by the love of Eppie, trading his security of money for real, unselfish love.

I don't want to compare myself with Silas Marner, but if I'm honest, I will admit the tendency to fear that God won't get us through each month unless I am very, very frugal. On the other hand, my husband tends toward greater abandonment to God's providence. (Many marriages, I've noticed, have one partner with each tendency!) Between my careful bookkeeping and Stockton's faith, God has gotten us through some very squeaky financial difficulties. Again, I have had to learn the hard way that worrying about money is a worthless investment in death.

God provides. Whether we fear He won't, or whether we feel certain He will, God does pull us through the tight places. The choice is ours—to live in fear or in trust. In retrospect, after many years of pinched pennies and tears at the end of the month, I have seen God's hand in our finances. I am not "cured" of this insecurity, though I am better. I know at a deeper level that true security is not in the bank, but in the assurance that God will take care of us.

Another literary example of someone trying to use money to find security is Jay Gatsby in F. Scott Fitzgerald's *The Great Gatsby*. Spurned as a young man by Daisy because he wasn't wealthy, Gatsby proceeds to make a fortune and builds a mansion right across the river from Daisy and her husband. He gives huge, elaborate, wild parties, hoping to lure her over to his house. Eventually, Gatsby does remeet his old flame, but Daisy is incapable of giving him the love he so desperately seeks, in spite of his house and his fortune, and a chifforobe filled with shirts they fling, together, around the room.

Many times we, too, fall for the illusion that money, or a big house, or a yellow roadster will give us the security we seek and the esteem of others. *The Great Gatsby* is an American classic precisely because it hits us where we live. Thousands of ads reach out to grab us every week from billboards, radio, TV, and magazines, trying to seduce us into believing that money will make us happy and feel secure. With such a barrage of propaganda, no wonder we have trouble with money. No wonder so many of the baby boomers' credit cards are maxed out. No wonder we place stock in things instead of God.

Still, the lesson is painfully obvious. Every time we feel tempted to find security in our finances or our belongings, we must fight the temptation. God brought us into the world naked, and He loves us whether we wear rags or designer clothes. Every time I'm tempted to worship financial security instead of God, I remember Gatsby, who ended up virtually friendless, floating facedown in his swimming pool.

Big houses do not win friends. Money does not make us any more important than we already are. Rich people are not better people. Wealth does not make us happy. Americans have been sold a bill of goods when we believe things will bring us peace and security.

Another example highlights what can happen when we worship money as a means of security. Some parents, like a man I once heard of, give their children too much in an unhealthy way. I don't know whether Mr. Smith was trying to buy his daughters' love, or whether he simply didn't know that his overgiving was ruining his children. Nevertheless, the effect was disastrous. Both his daughters married into "society" in the East, and from his tiny apartment in a small Texas town he slowly starved himself to death, almost literally, while his daughters drove Jaguars and Mercedes and bought designer clothes. By the time their father died penniless, the girls had turned into bottomless pits of greed. They could never rest secure until they had the latest style in clothes, the latest car, the latest whatever.

When we worship finances as a means to security, we are never satisfied. Even if we achieve our financial goal— our personal benchmark of security—strangely, it isn't enough. We need more in order to feel really secure. At some point, we have to recognize that we are in a cruel trap. The only feeling generated by collecting bigger and better things is a greater need for bigger and better things. That warm feeling of peace and security lies in a different direction altogether, along a different path.

I am not denigrating wealth here. John Wesley always said, "Make all you can; save all you can; give all you can." What I am talking about is using money as a foundation of security. God is our security. To confuse the two is a downward spiral into greed and insecurity. Scripture says that it is difficult—not impossible—for a wealthy person to enter the Kingdom of Heaven. The question is our fundamental attitude toward our possessions: Where have we placed our trust?

One man made a fortune in the oil business, then lost his money. However, his spiritual growth corresponded to his material decline. Unlike some of his fellow millionaires in a tough business, he resisted cheating and corruption and learned to place his value on higher things. The life of this man makes a strong statement against the culture's assumption that the worth of the person is directly related to financial standing. His story also counters the leftover Puritan ideal that the better you are, the more the Lord will bless you, making you steward over great wealth. His message seems to be, "It's what you do with what you've got, not how much you've got."

God loves us, rich or poor. We cannot let our faith ride

SEDUCTION OF THE LESSER GODS

on the false assumption that wealth is a sign of God's blessing and poverty is a sign of His displeasure. Or vice versa.
Just because we are poor does not mean we are holy. Our
security as Christians must be in the cross and the promises of God's love, regardless of our financial state of affairs.

Money can be a tricky demon, and we fall right into the
hands of the enemy when we place our trust in wealth instead of God. Worry corrodes the quality of life, whereas
dependence on God for our material needs opens a great
pantry of peace and assurance.

SAFETY FROM HARM

Mel Gibson, speaking as the Scottish hero William Wallace
in *Braveheart*, responded to those who feared for his life,
"Everyone dies. The important thing is to die well." These
were difficult words for him because he was literally gutted
while still alive, as his enemies attempted to make him re-
cant his political position. He died a heroic death when he
refused to succumb to the pain, shouting "Freedom!" before his executioner mercifully cut off his head.

William Wallace's calm acceptance of the bald, un-
changeable fact that "everyone dies" allowed him to take
enormous risks in his noble pursuit of freedom. As
Christians, we, too, need to accept death. For though we
all die sooner or later, death is not the final word. Christ

has conquered this treacherous enemy, and given us everlasting life! The important thing for Christians is not that we die well, but that we accept this unspeakably marvelous gift—so that no matter how we die, we will in fact live past the moment of mortal harm.

Any nightly newscast reveals that we live in a dangerous and harmful world. Violence is on the rise. Gang members drive by and shoot each other, along with innocent victims. Drug-related murders and robberies increase year after year. In spite of tougher laws, drunk drivers continue to kill. Natural disasters wipe out whole communities. And on and on and on.

Though we think our era is especially dangerous, the truth is 'twas ever thus. Life has always been hazardous. Vandals, Vikings, Goths, and disease used to wipe out whole cities at a time. People have always killed each other. When I was in college, public television did a series based on Robert Graves's *I, Claudius*. This historical story showed clearly that poisonings and stabbings among the aristocracy in the Roman Empire were commonplace. Even in the Bible, getting a foothold in the Promised Land was not without wholesale bloodshed.

Because science has found so many cures for deadly diseases, because our court system is a reliable dispenser of law and justice, because our people have a high level of education, and because our country was founded on Christian principles, we think we should be exempt from the perils of life. Not so, unfortunately. Our precarious existence inevitably ends in death. Because of the fall, we no longer cavort safely in the garden prepared for us by God. We live east of Eden, where serpents continue to lure us into danger.

With this understanding as a starting point, we can fully appreciate the astonishing fact that many of us live fulfilling lives until we die of old age. Miracles also happen on the earth, and we are often protected by angels. We are not doomed to terror and fear. When Jesus is our security, we can walk through the world knowing that we are safe from ultimate harm: though we will die, yet we will live. This knowledge actually frees us for a happier, more carefree existence on earth. We can enjoy the gifts blooming each day of our lives.

Three of my relatives were murdered in a robbery-gone-wrong, a tragedy that taught me many important things. Sometimes we cannot escape violence. Sometimes we are innocent victims of others' sin. And yet their deaths taught me another important lesson as well: death does not have the last word. I struggled for several years, wondering why they had not been protected physically from harm, before I realized that sometimes God allows earthly protection, and sometimes He brings us home.

However wonderful our lives on earth might be, heaven is always the greater reward. In Philippians, Paul is torn between wanting to die and be with Christ and needing to continue to live in the flesh to finish his earthly job. "My desire is to depart and be with Christ, for that is far better" (Phil. 1:23).

This is not an easy thing for me to write, and I'm not sure I've worked out the problem of God's protection yet. All I know is that if we place our security in God, He will somehow redeem it, even when we die an earthly death.

We need to do the best we can to avert harm—why tempt fate? As responsible people, we need to protect ourselves as best we can: wear our seat belts, install security systems, have our children inoculated. The theological rub comes when people still die in car wrecks, even using seat belts. We realize then that our safety nets sometimes have holes; our safeguards are not the ultimate answer. The fact is, we are not safe from death. It will happen, and it will happen to us. Our real security must be in Jesus. Only in Him can we live in true safety.

SECURITY AS HUMAN BEINGS

Finally, there is the problem of our security as human beings. The twelve-step recovery movement has done much good in this area, enabling us to reclaim our wholeness and our right to feel secure as God's children. We no longer need to cower as shame-filled, abused people, tremulously afraid that we don't deserve God's blessings. Jesus has given us as human beings a rock to stand on. This security in our personhood is one of the gifts of the cross.

Our human condition is that we are jettisoned from the womb into an ocean of needs and insecurities. As infants, our needs are met by being held and fed, and our insecurities are allayed at the same time. As we grow physically, our sense of worth (or nonworth) also develops. Where does the sense of worth come from? Parents who teach their children that they are precious children of God lead their youngsters straight to the source of all security. However, many parents can't teach this to their children. They've either lost this belief about themselves, or their own parents never gave them this priceless message. Instead, children flounder in a sea of insecurity, clinging to various rafts as lifesavers: looks, intelligence, family background, money, athletic prowess, or whatever it is that gives a measure of approval or satisfaction.

As we cling to these unstable rafts for worth, what we don't realize is that God's love is a continent of secure land with a sturdy dock along the coastline, a home port for our souls tossed about in this ocean of uncertainty. Only when we are safely docked there can we be free of the churning waves, the seasickness, the exhausting effort of trying to maintain our self-worth by clinging to tiny rafts that can barely buoy our self-esteem.

I spent many of my teen and young adult years clinging to various life rafts: I learned not to walk into a lunchroom without a friend; not to speak up in class; not to sing above a murmur at church; not to buy clothes except certain "in" styles. Friends, clothes, good manners, a quiet demeanor—these things buoyed the insecurity I felt as a human being.

What I've learned since is that God wants us to be ourselves, to be secure in our own skins. He gave us personalities and gifts, and He wants us to glisten radiantly. When we are free of our false inhibitions, we are free to love each other and to live full and happy lives. Security is like electricity. A person secure in God's love becomes a conduit of blessings, and those around them bask in the emanations of wholeness radiating from them.

Conversely, insecurity also spreads like electricity, shocking us unpleasantly. This phenomenon works well, unfortunately, in the classroom. Most people have suffered from professors who sneeringly put down students to make themselves seem smarter or more powerful.

The classic example of an insecure person is Adolf Hitler. I'm a World War II buff and a docent at the World War II Air Force Museum here. In my opinion, Adolf Hitler is the most extreme twentieth-century example of failed humanness. Much of the destruction he caused stemmed from his inability to deal with his own insecurities.

History tells us Hitler was insecure about his family (he was born illegitimately); insecure about his homeland (he was born Austrian, not German); insecure about his race (he may have had some Jewish blood); insecure about his military prowess (he was a mere corporal in World War I, though he considered himself a military genius); insecure about his artistic abilities (he was rejected not once but twice by the Art Academy in Vienna).

The great craving and passion of Hitler's early life was to be an artist, and I have often wondered what would have happened had the Academy accepted and fostered Hitler's artistic gift. Could the destruction of Europe have been avoided by acceptance of his architectural sketches? One can only speculate.

The cultural climate and Germany's humiliation after World War I only fired Hitler's personal insecurities. His ruthlessness, lack of social conscience, and lust for total power, combined with these insecurities, produced the greatest destruction the world has ever seen. Though Hitler may be an extreme example, the point remains the same: Until we feel comfortable in our own skins, we are likely to make life uncomfortable for ourselves and those around us.

A more everyday example is the case of Rick, a seventeen-year-old boy just beginning to outgrow his gangliness and acne. Shy and insecure, Rick forgot his inhibitions on the basketball court; unfortunately, he found himself tongue-tied with girls and decided it was easier to ignore them in the halls than to make a fool out of himself trying to make conversation.

When it came time for the annual athletic banquet, Rick anguished over a date. His father encouraged him to ask Marie, a cute girl in his math class. After three days of putting off the call, he finally asked Marie, and she accepted. The date went fine, and although Rick felt awkward much of the time, he wanted to ask her out again. The next day at school, he spotted Marie next to the library door, talking with a group of friends. Not particularly outgoing herself, she gave him a shy smile. As Rick approached the cluster of girls, his insecurity overtook him, and he walked past without saying hi.

That night, Rick's father asked if he'd seen Marie. "Yeah," mumbled Rick.

"Did you say hello?" asked his father.

"Well," Rick hemmed and hawed. "Not exactly."

His father looked at him. "Why not?"

"I was too self-conscious," replied Rick miserably.

His father sighed. "Listen to yourself. 'Self-conscious.' Analyze that word. Conscious of self. Not conscious of anybody else. You probably hurt Marie's feelings because you were thinking only of yourself. Insecurity is just another form of selfishness."

Many times insecurity comes across as arrogance, in both teens and adults. We do not need to suffer from insecurity. Because God loves us so much, we all have the potential to live with our souls safe, secure in the knowledge and love of God. As people we emit emotion; we cannot help spreading what is at our center. The more power we have, the greater our influence for good or evil. If we cannot get rid of the insecurity, we may end up like little Hitlers.

Insecurity lies at the root of much human unhappiness, including envy, lust, covetousness, hatred, and fear. If we are happy being ourselves, we are more likely to let others be happy. We can rest content with what we have; we can rejoice in others' blessings instead of trying to get even, making snide comments, building our empires by wiping out others'.

The process of gaining security sounds easier than it is. It has taken me twenty years to gain the courage to wear the clothes I want, to sing with gusto at church, to let myself feel loved by God, to feel confident in my own skin—and I still have setbacks. Paul Tillich's sermon "You Are Accepted" describes the salvation we experience, the security we feel when we accept the divine acceptance of us:

> Grace strikes us when we are in great pain and restlessness. It strikes us when we walk through the dark valley of meaninglessness and empty life. It strikes us when we feel that our separation is deeper than usual, because we feel we have violated another life, . . . It strikes us when, year after year, the longed-for perfection of life does not appear, when old compulsions reign within us as they have for decades, when despair destroys all joy and courage. Sometimes at that moment a wave of light breaks into our darkness, and it is as though a voice were saying: "You are accepted, accepted by that which is greater than you. . . . Do not seek for anything; do not perform anything; do not intend anything. Simply accept the fact that you are accepted!" [2]

Our lives are a gift to ourselves. God made us, and He wants us to rejoice in our being. Delighting in our personhood is not the same as inflating our egos. Big egos are a result of fluffing ourselves out of insecurity. When we live in gratitude for our own lives and our gifts, then and only then can we freely love others.

THE SECURITY OF DAVID

The story of David and Goliath illustrates the great security God gives. As my son Jase pointed out while studying the puzzle of David and Goliath he'd finished: "Why did Goliath feel like he had to wear so much armor? He could have squushed David like a bug." True. We are sometimes like Goliath, putting on armor, to keep ourselves safe from harm.

In contrast, David ought to have been insecure on many accounts. Smaller than his giant opponent, he should have been worried that he would be wiped out in a matter of minutes. He should have been insecure about the quality of his weaponry. He should have been insecure about his ability to perform under extreme pressure.

Instead, David placed all his faith in God. "The LORD who delivered me from the paw of the lion and from the paw of the bear, will deliver me from the hand of this Philistine" (1 Sam. 17:37). David took what precautions he could, gathering five smooth stones, and faced Goliath "in the name of the LORD of hosts" (1 Sam. 17:45).

We can learn from David as we travel this insecure journey of life. Whether we worry about safety from harm, about financial difficulties, about where we will live, or about who we are, all our insecurities dissolve when we face life as David faced Goliath. The same God who protected David protects us; and David's descendant, Jesus Christ, has saved us from the ultimate enemy, death. We may try our best to buttress our fortunes against the winds of fate, but the psalmist is right: "Only in Thee can we live in safety" (Ps. 4:8).

The more secure we feel in the love of God, the greater becomes our ability to love others as well as ourselves. Just as God is the true source of security, He is also the true source of love.

Chapter 4	# LOVE

Love begins to be a demon the moment he begins to be a god.
— C.S. LEWIS, *The Four Loves*

John sits in his office among familiar, urgent clutter, watching the blizzard outside his window when the receptionist buzzes with a hint of panic in her voice. He quickly downs one of the mints designed to help him quit smoking and within seconds learns that his daughter on the opposite coast has been hit by a drunk driver. She isn't expected to live through the night.

John makes it halfway across the country to Chicago O'Hare, where the prim, nervous woman at the ticket counter says, "The runways won't be cleared until tomorrow morning. Nothing's taking off until 6:00 A.M."

So he spends another $100 he doesn't really have and opens the door to a dark motel room smelling of whatever disinfectant was used to erase any traces of past human life in the room. It's so late, he doesn't even hang up his clothes. After he calls the hospital and finds out his daughter is still in critical condition, he curls up on the bedspread with his shoes still on. The image of his only child appears—her face cut by the windshield, her body broken. Then he remembers her dimples, her big-eyed smile the time she took all the household sheets to school to cut up for angel costumes for the students who couldn't afford their own.

He stares at the swag lamp in the corner. He lights a cigarette, realizing that within a radius of 100 miles there must be ten million people, but with the exception of his old roommate's crazy cousin Henrietta, he doesn't know a single person he can call. As he lies propped against the pillows, his soul—that floppy bag where he's stored things too precious, too frightening to talk about—starts to rip away from the lining of his body, and he fears he will be left, if he survives the night, with nothing in there but black, fetid air.

When he squashes out his cigarette in the happy face ashtray beaming "Have a nice day," his eye catches on the red Bible with cracked gold letters placed on the bedside table by the Gideons. The Bible. He had almost forgotten the message of comfort scattered among the foreign names and stilted turns of phrase.

"God," he says, then stops. He can't continue because he cannot say aloud what he is thinking in his heart of hearts: If God takes his only child away from him, he can never pray to Him again.

John gets up and forages around among the toiletries, finding at last a little something the doctor prescribed for stress. He takes three. He goes back to the bed, this time taking off his clothes and crawling under the covers.

"God," he says again into the strange room. The only sound is the heater shutting off. He cannot let go of the hope God is somehow in that motel room with him.

Before flicking off the light, he opens the red Gideon Bible. Flipping through, he sees Adam and Eve, Noah, the Tower of Babel; then he sees an old, old man carrying his son up the side of the mountain. "Oh, no," he says aloud. "No." He closes the book.

Lying alone in the dark, he pictures the old man tying his little boy to an altar, the boy looking at him with frightened yet trustful eyes, while tears fill up the deep cracks in the old man's face. John thinks of his daughter tied by tubes to another potential deathbed.

The old man Abraham arranges the sticks for the burnt offering around the boy. He lifts his hand with a knife. Then, when he is almost crazed with silent pain, right before he hears the rustle of the ram in the bushes, the old man whispers straight into John's heart, "You must love the Giver more than the gift."

At that moment, John knew that the love of God was more powerful than his love for his daughter. Somehow things would work out all right.

ON THE MOUNTAIN

The story of Abraham and Isaac on the mountain always moves me deeply. Maybe it's an overidentification with Abraham and Sarah. Like them, my husband and I waited a long time before God blessed us with children; but unlike them, I would have been tempted to hide my children in a large footlocker and take the first plane to Siberia before I'd lead either of them up the brambled mountain path, to cut their throats and give them back to God as a sacrifice.

Other Bible stories, too, speak of terrible sacrifices of loved ones. The holy innocents killed by Herod, for example. I can't imagine what those mothers felt when the soldiers broke into their homes and murdered their children.

On the one hand, we are commanded to love one another. The Ten Commandments tell us to honor our parents; Leviticus 19:18 tells us to love our neighbors as ourselves. In John 15:12 (and elsewhere), Jesus commands His disciples and us to "love one another as I have loved you." This love is what shows the world that we are Christ's disciples.

However, in the Gospel of Matthew, Jesus gives us another, more troubling command, underscoring the point of the Abraham story. We cannot afford to ignore this message in favor of the easier injunction to love people. "He who loves father or mother more than me is not worthy of me; and he who loves son or daughter more than me is not worthy of me" (Matt. 10:37). Here Matthew actually softened the blow, choosing to smooth over the harshness of the Semitic word "hate" which Luke kept in his version of the same saying (14:26).

What kind of a God are we dealing with here, anyway? Out of one side of His mouth, He commands us to love and honor our family and neighbors, and out of the other side, to hate them. What does this contradiction mean?

Actually, it's not a contradiction. Jesus is warning us against idolatry, against the temptation to love anybody more than Him—warning against what would have been my inclination, had I been Abraham, to hide my children instead of offering them to God. The point made in both the Old and New Testaments is this: Love God first and the other loves will work themselves out.

My son gave me a white, scented candle that burns on my desk when I write. I love that candle. An aroma of gardenia rises like incense, and I think of my precious, playful child when I watch the flame happily licking the air. As much as I enjoy and appreciate the candle, though, I do not love it more than I love my son.

By the same token, God gives us children, spouses, parents, sisters, brothers, and friends as candles in our lives. These other human beings flicker around us, providing light and warmth and love, but we are clearly warned not to love the gifts more than the giver. This is one of the hardest truths in the Bible.

When Jesus tells His disciples, "If any one comes to me and does not hate his father and mother and wife and children and brothers and sisters, yes, and even his own life, he cannot be my disciple" (Luke 14:26), He is setting out the terms of discipleship. I picture Jesus talking to the twelve—puzzled, as usual—seated under a eucalyptus tree, Peter picking at the grass wondering what He meant this time. Jesus was always turning things upside down.

In the biblical context, maybe Jesus sensed that most of the twelve sitting around Him would be killed for His sake. Maybe He knew that each one would have to make an ultimate choice—family or Him.

Likewise, in the early church, Christians often had to choose between Jesus and their pagan or Jewish family ties—a choice that sometimes meant a martyr's death. Jesus' admonition to His disciples thus took on a frightening immediacy. In order to fulfill their Christian destiny, the disciples had to "hate" their families, especially if the family tempted them away from their new and tender faith.

Love

THE GREAT COMMANDMENT

Jesus resolves the apparent contradiction between honoring and hating parents and family when He combines Leviticus 19:18 and Deuteronomy 6:5 into one new, two-part commandment. The breathtaking freshness of this conjunction is lost on us today, but consider the scene. One of the religious and intellectual elite—a lawyer in Luke and Matthew and a scribe in Mark—struts up in his fancy robe, approaches Jesus, and tries to trick Him, asking, "Which commandment is the greatest?" Jesus, as usual, outwits the interrogator, who, in Mark, admits in spite of himself the wisdom of such an astonishing answer. "'You shall love the Lord your God with all your heart, and with all your soul, and with all your mind, and with all your strength.' The second is this, 'You shall love your neighbor as yourself'" (Mark 12:30–31). The two become one! Indissoluble. This means that loving ourselves and our neighbors fully is bound up with loving God first.

In other words, God's love is the great tree onto which we graft our earthly loves; God's love nourishes the bonds we feel toward those He has placed intimately in our lives. Trying to love our neighbors and family without loving God is like hanging ornaments on a dead Christmas tree.

Then why is loving God first so difficult? Is it just because we desperately need approval and affection from people "with skin on"? Do we find it difficult to trust Him because He calls people we love home to Him before we're ready to relinquish them?

In the last decade, I've dealt intensely with the dysfunction of my family of origin. In addition, during one four-and-a-half-year period, Stockton and I lost eleven loved ones through death. These two processes of grief and separation have forced me to examine my definition of love and taught me a great deal about the false notions I have worshiped instead of God.

WHAT REAL LOVE ISN'T

No one in all of literature, even Shakespeare, defines love better than Paul does in 1 Corinthians 13. In many senses we read this poetic passage and weep because we can't hope to live up to its purity, at least in our natural condition. This passage describes Jesus and His perfect, self-giving, sacrificial love, an agape we are called to strive for but cannot attain without His grace. As I read about the gong and cymbal, I hear the tinny clanging in my own life and remember the irritation I feel when I hurry my laggardly children out the door when they are late to school in the mornings, or when I argue with Stockton over something trivial like emptying the trash. Paul's passage gives us the gold standard of love, and part of our job as Christians is to examine our own lives for the counterfeits we try to pass off as authentic.

Love

God is love. We know that. But the opposite is not necessarily true. Love is not always God. Literature has expressed
this in different ways. One writer says that we cannot pray
to God without praying to Love, but we can pray to Love
without praying to God.[1] When we pray to love instead of
to God, we feel that both love and God have failed us when
our loved ones die, or leave us, or grow cold in their affection. Earthly love sours, and it feels as though God doesn't
love us anymore either. As one of my friends said, "Because
I confused the love of God with the love of my mom, when
she filed for divorce and left my dad, I felt that God, too,
had taken off in a Mercedes-Benz, leaving us all by the side
of the road in a cloud of dust."

Real love doesn't abandon you. Mothers might. Lovers
might. Friends might. Children might. But God doesn't.
This is what I learned in the dead of night. Jesus Christ
comes to us, arms outstretched, as we struggle, sleepless,
on old brown couches; as we drink alone in bars; as we sit
in faded armchairs watching reruns on TV; as we make
love to the wrong people, pursue the wrong paths of happiness, stew in our self-made pots of resentment and fear.
Whether we return the embrace or not, Jesus Christ stands
with His arms open, day in and day out. Real love knows
us completely and forgives us completely.

Real love does not turn away, ever.

ↄ

We can't get something this great by loving other human beings first and foremost. Sooner or later people fail us (as we fail them) because they cannot love unconditionally. Part of our human makeup is that we cannot remove our selves and our needs when we attempt to love an other. Only Jesus' love has no hidden agendas.

In every association—not just romantic affairs of the heart or parent-child relationships—we as self, encounter and dance with an other, both lugging needs like backpacks. In casual contacts with, say, a grocery clerk, a letter carrier, or the young man in the next car at the stoplight, the relationship is not typically more complicated than a word or two, possibly a gesture. Nevertheless, every encounter contains the potential for grief or charity. When self encounters other, we either spread bits of love as described by Paul (kindness, patience, humility) or we infect the brief encounter with the opposite (arrogance, rudeness, jealousy).

By the same token, others unload their moods on us, which can make or break the next thirty minutes of our lives. If we are not grounded in God's love, we can easily let a rude clerk spoil the drive all the way home from the store. Or we can radiate our own irritation to the unknown human voice which (finally!) answers the telephone after we've suffered through seventeen automated menus on the 800 number we are trying to call. Love or nonlove is operative even in our smallest gestures as we drive, as we wait in line, as we walk through a seemingly uneventful day.

Real love doesn't allow sand in the grease of the machinery of human exchange.

—⟋⟍—

For more intimate and lasting relationships, the encounter between self and other becomes more complicated and entangled. Ideally, love is other focused; love delights in sacrificing so the loved one can be blessed. An example is the husband of one married couple I know, both professors. In a noble and sincere gesture, this man, without drawing attention to himself, unhesitatingly gave up his own potential appointment to a prestigious position so that his wife could be the one honored.

Love becomes less than love when self gets covetous, or when self lets the other get covetous. When a person becomes an object of desire, or a prize to be gained, won, or possessed, love is not love. Friendship with someone we consider famous, a date with a well-known beauty—these relationships are not based on love but on the reward we think we'll get by association.

American writer Ralph Waldo Emerson states that, in "the last analysis, love is only the reflection of a man's own worthiness from other men."[2] If this were a true state of affairs, then God's love would not be possible because we could never transcend our own needs in seeking love. Like barnacles, we would be constantly searching for other people to stick onto so we could get what we need from them.

Unfortunately, it seems impossible to enter into relationship with an other without carrying at least a small backpack of our own needs; still, we are not stuck at the level of selfish, reflective love. We might start out striving to attain Paul's qualities of kindness and patience so that the other will provide us with a good reflection of ourselves. But as we practice the behavior in Paul's list, pretty soon, with God's grace, we live into the characteristics for the sake of the other person. Though the ancient Roman poet Ovid in his *Art of Love* refers to romantic love, the principle works with Paul's kind of love as well: "Often the pretender begins to love truly and ends by becoming what he feigned to be."[3] This principle works best when we love God first.

Real love, then, is not seeking a mirror for our selves in the love of another.

⌒

Misuse of the self/other relationship is played out in dramas as violent as wife beatings and rape, or in circumstances as subtle as sending a card so the recipient will think well of me. A healthy self/other relationship presupposes a healthy respect for both self as well as the other. In fact, most abuses occur because the self is diminished, and this pain is taken out on the other.

In 1961, the Irish-French playwright Samuel Beckett wrote a classic play entitled *Happy Days* (not to be confused with The Fonz of TV fame!). In an unusual setting, a woman named Winnie is buried up to her waist in a mound of dirt, and talks to her husband, Willie, nonstop throughout the entire first act. Willie speaks thirty-seven words compared to the ocean of his wife's verbiage. At one point, Winnie asks her husband a poignant question: "Was I ever lovable?"[4] making the distinction between the other, more superficial question, "Did you ever love me?" Willie doesn't answer either question.

Winnie's question—am I lovable?—is at the heart of most of our quests for love. The question "Do you love me?" is about the emotions of the other and whether the other chooses to take us on as an object of affection; the question "Am I lovable?" has to do with the essence of our being. As humans, we tend to answer the second question for each other, leaving the first question dangling. God's love is what comforts us at the deeper level. "I made you," He answers us. "I died for you. Yes, you are lovable."

Real love does not leave the deeper question unanswered.

Another way we confuse real love with false love is obvious to everyone except teenagers and men and women in the throes of mid-life crises. Songs like "Some Enchanted

Evening" from *South Pacific* aid and abet our misplaced longing. Across a crowded room, we spot a person of the opposite sex, and what we call love suddenly surges through our veins; in one glance our blood turns to wine and our hormones jangle in new (or forgotten) harmonies.

Those of us not in mid-life crises see this mating dance for what it is. However, for those blindly smitten people, part of the power of this eros love is the seemingly inevitable linking of lust and agape love. People in this trancelike state seem unable to distinguish between the developed landscape of a carefully tended garden and the flamboyant blooms of fierce attraction to another human being. I have seen too many middle-aged people, both men and women, abandon Paul's boring old injunction that real love endures all things and jump right into a fresh and titillating relationship, destroying a spouse and children, telling themselves not that they want to satisfy bodily drives, but that at last they have found the "real thing."

Paul does not say that agape love is supposed to be as thrilling as eros. Fortunately, God knows our desire for racing hearts and gives us a way that we don't have to give up our need for excitement; in fact, in the context of marriage, our physical pleasure grows in direct proportion to the growth of the kind of love Paul describes. The reverse is also true—a satisfying and delicious roll in the hay does wonders in helping us endure all things. By choosing to stick out a commitment and focusing on the kind of love described in 1 Corinthians, romance has a chance to return. Problems sprout when we start praying to the wrong kind of love instead of to God.

Real love is not lust.

Real love is also not nagging, criticizing, abusing, or ignoring a mate so intensely that he or she is driven to satisfy the need for love with someone outside the marriage.

Love is an act of will: listening to someone when we are bored, keeping that perfectly couched comeback to ourselves, letting old Mrs. Jones win the argument over something unimportant, biting our tongues instead of reminding others of our triumphs, hearing out our spouse one more time on the same old saw (and hoping he or she will return the favor). Love is not waiting to feel good before plunging into these and other unselfish acts, but rather love is the decision to behave a certain way even when we feel like Ms. or Mr. Grump.

If we are to love people as Christ commanded us, then we must be willing not to plant our feet on our side of the fence, howling self-righteous epithets to the other side, but rather to climb over the fence and see what the world looks like from the other point of view. Many times resentments evaporate and hatreds fizzle when we understand why people are the way they are. Loving someone is a process of untangling the complicated threads of their personhood from their point of view, not ours. Loving someone is holding our own needs in abeyance while exploring why they did the apparently hurtful thing to us. The process takes patience, kindness, hope, endurance . . . well, 1 Corinthians 13 says it all.

BELONGING

One of our children's books concludes a beautiful and heart-warming story, "Adoption means belonging." Since we all have been adopted by God, I think it's safe to stretch the definition to, "Real love means belonging to God." We all seek that warm hearth where our battered souls can finally come home to a place where we belong.

The word *belonging*, though, has some interesting connotations that need to be explored before we jump right in and claim the definition as ours. "Belonging" is a double-edged word. On the one hand, belonging suggests that we have the proper qualifications to be a member of a club or group. We have passed some sort of criterion. We are part of an in-crowd, invited to participate where others may not be included. Though this slant on the term may appeal to our elitist tendencies, the criterion for membership in God's Kingdom has nothing to do with our worth. We belong to God because Jesus paid the price for our sins on the cross.

The Old English *gelang* suggests a dependency in be-longing. We are beholden to those to whom we belong. Belonging implies a certain giving up of independence, a willingness to lean on someone who will in turn protect and take care of us. When we relinquish our lives to Jesus Christ, we can rest knowing that our lives are in good hands.

However, on earth we must be careful to whom we be-long. The other side of "belonging" implies possession. It is one small step from a snug "belonging" to being owned, treated like a thing. Children have no choice to whom they belong, and daily tragedies occur because parents do not always treat their children as the precious jewels they are. As adults, we can choose to whom we give ourselves in trust and love. But we, too, must be sure to belong to God first before we let ourselves "belong" to anyone else.

Finally, through the centuries poets have all spoken of the kind of love that transcends death. When we belong to God, loving Him first, and the people we love also belong to God, then we do not lose them when they die. The rela-tionship is simply interrupted until we, too, finish our earthly business. When I lost so many of my loved ones, I told my spiritual advisor that it was as if the web of love woven among all of us were being lifted into another di-mension, anchor by anchor, person by person. The connections were still intact, just temporarily invisible—and that when it came my turn to die, I would find the network ready and waiting for me, in the larger network of the love of

God. Knowing this didn't stop the pain of missing all of them, but as the months passed, the consolation became more real than the loss.

Eighteenth-century English poet Alexander Pope wrote a poem called "Eloisa to Abelard," taken from the story of Pierre Abelard, considered the founder of the University of Paris, and Heloise, his beautiful and learned pupil. In the poem, Pope warns us against valuing relationships with people over relationship with God.

> O Death, all-eloquent! you only prove
> What dust we doat on, when 'tis man we love.[5]

We dote on dust when we worship earthly love—but what eternal treasures are in store for us and for our loved ones when we worship the God of love Himself!

Chapter 5

URGENCY

Be still, and know that I am God.
—PSALM 46:10

Still in shock, Lawrence watched the funeral director zip the body bag over his wife's face. Irrationally he thought, "Don't do that! She can't breathe." Silently, the men carried Lily out the door and loaded her into the wagon.

When the funeral home people had gone, Lawrence sat down on the edge of the rumpled bed where just a few minutes ago, it seemed, he had rolled over and discovered a cold dead hand instead of his wife's warm embrace and her irritating, "Rise and shine!" The pastor would be here soon, and a cadre of women from the Consolation Committee bringing food and tears of sympathy.

By the side of his wife's bed, Lawrence noticed her daily list of things to do. "Buy dog food. Call Marion. Find a substitute for the museum. Write Susan. Beauty—IMMED. Bake bread for do tonight. Smooth Pat's ruffled feathers. Change bulb in dining room (find special lights—Dan's Lighting?)." Every night for twenty-seven years his wife had written out a list for the following day. She'd wake up brightly and begin attacking the list in a frenzy.

Beauty—IMMED. What was that?

The coroner said her heart had stopped in her sleep. Had she been under stress lately? No more so than the last twenty-seven years. Had she been getting regular exercise? She'd quit aerobics five years ago because she didn't have time. His wife had worshiped her list of things to do, and aerobics took away from her ability to cross every item off before she crawled into bed at night.

Beauty. Beauty shop? IMMED. Immediately? Probably. But what was the rush? Now he would never know what she meant to do, and the IMMED stared at him in grim irony. Maybe if she hadn't always been in a hurry, she could have lived to finish her list one more day.

God's time is not our time. God provides us lesson after lesson, trying to teach us that patience is truly a Christian virtue. Yet time and time again, we live our lives governed by a pressing list of things to do. More than anything else, urgency keeps our lives in chains, keeps our stomachs in knots, keeps our hearts fluttering erratically—and keeps our souls at a shouting distance, instead of a whispering distance, from God. Most of us need reminding that eternity is not measured with a stopwatch and that, like Lily, allowing urgency to rule our lives can literally kill us.

TIME

Though our constitution says that all Americans are created equal, we all know that, in practical terms, this is not true. Theoretically, yes. Politically, yes. However, some are born with IQs of 150; some are born into wealthy homes; some are born to caring parents who have time to lavish on their children; some are born in perfect health. Others are not so fortunate in all these regards. Though gifts and circumstances vary greatly from person to person, the great equalizer in our country is time. True, we do not know how many days we will be given—life spans vary greatly. But as long as we're alive, every single person is given twenty-four hours a day—no more, no less. With slight variations accounting for irregularities in the earth's motion, the number of hours allotted to human beings per day has been the same since the beginning of time itself.

So why is our culture so tyrannized by the urgent? What has happened to our perception of time that so many of us feel our lives are in a vise? We cannot worship God the way we would like, or do many of the other activities important to us, because we simply don't have time. Instead we allow the sense of urgency to become a god to us.

Meet Mr. and Mrs. Average Citizen, living in the Holy Land during the time of Jesus. Mr. Citizen says to his wife, "Honey, I'll be home for supper." Sometime near the end of the day, Mrs. Citizen pulls fresh bread out of the stone oven, and if her husband hasn't been delayed by running into friends on his way back from fishing on the Sea of Galilee, he strolls in the door whenever he gets there. What time is it? Who knows? It's the end of the day, closer to 5:00 in the winter and more like 8:00 in the summer. But who's counting? Who can? Maybe there's a sundial in the middle of Capernaum, but in the Average Citizen's home, time is approximate at best, divided into dawn, morning, noon, afternoon, evening, and night. Mr. Citizen has fished for as long as he can see, and Mrs. Citizen has gone to market and cooked, too, as long as daylight allows.

A millenium and a half later, Mr. and Mrs. Average Citizen live in a town with a big clock in the center of the town square. Galileo has discovered the pendulum. This clock in the center of town bongs every hour, so Mr. Citizen (because he lives within sound of the main clock) can tell his wife, "Honey, I'll be home for supper before the clock strikes 6." Though the measurement of time has become more precise, life—agriculture and commerce, as well as life around the house—is still primarily based on daylight. Farmers sow and harvest crops from sunup to sunset; stores in town conduct business during daylight hours; public entertainment, such as drama, takes place in the afternoon; and in general, the rhythm of life is still closely tied to the rhythm of the earth.

Two centuries later in Victorian England, Mr. Citizen buys a watch he can carry around with him in his pocket. Mrs. Citizen also has a clock in her own home. They can arrange to be more specific about meeting for dinner. "I won't be home until 6:10," Mr. Citizen tells his wife. Civilization is taking control of the earth's natural rhythms. Lamps now light the streets, and the theater has gaslights, so public entertainment and activities encroach into the night. People expect banks, shops, and businesses to open and close at a certain specific time. As communications increase, the pace of life also increases, and the measurement of time becomes more precise and demanding.

In twentieth-century America, much has changed, especially the pace of life. Mrs. Citizen now calls her husband's car phone from her office and says, "Honey, I'm running late at work. When you get home, will you put the frozen dinners in the microwave?" We carry on life and commerce twenty-four hours a day—on the internet, on television, in late-night entertainment, in twenty-four-hour 800 numbers. Airports and whole cities offer no difference between night and day. We are far removed from the earth's natural rhythms, and our artificial constructs of existence are killing us inside.

We all know this. We all fight the pace of life. The tragedy of the late twentieth century is that we must fight the invisible forces that whip us like a pack of devils through our days. With all of our time-saving devices, we have less time. We have either filled up the vacuum with stuff we're not really interested in, or our time-saving devices don't really save us time. Either way, we're in a spiritual prison, while the walls of our lives slowly crunch us like a giant trash compactor.

How do we allow ourselves to get in this tight place?

OUR INVISIBLE CULTURAL PRESSURES

One reason historical analysis is easier than analysis of current events is that present-tense lenses make so much of our lives invisible. We literally cannot delineate the forces that control our lives because they are too close to us and are too much a part of the texture of what we think we must accept for survival.

For instance, if we participate in television at all, even in self-monitored selections, we have to accept the fact that, like little white mice in scientists' laboratories, our attention spans have been conditioned into thirty-second, sixty-second, ten- and twenty-minute segments. The industry has trained us to accept the tidbits fed to us in increments of time studied and proven for maximum effectiveness. A few channels, such as public broadcasting, respect our (diminishing) desire *and ability* to settle in for a longer spell. Otherwise, television feeds us information in controlled pieces; we have lost the ability to consume information at our own rates.

Recently, I got caught at a fast-food chain as the high school let its students out for lunch. Dismayed, I viewed the line. Getting lunch would now take a full seven minutes instead of the usual two. I had allowed myself only one extra minute for unforseen trouble between picking up the tacos and speeding to my engagement at twelve-thirty. Quickly, I chose to careen through the less-crowded drive-through next door, but I still arrived late to my engagement. In the meantime, my body experienced mild signals of stress and irritation because I hate to be late.

Problem: I had allowed three minutes because *I could do it in three minutes.* I had grabbed lunch many times in three minutes on the way to this weekly engagement. I had been trained, again like a laboratory mouse, to respond to my environment with the predictability of Pavlov's dog. In a fast-paced world, we expect and rely on the speed promised us by ads and by our experience. Then, when something goes wrong—a long line, or a broken down car, or a phone call on the way out the door—our lives are suddenly stressful because we haven't budgeted enough time for things to go wrong.

Our culture doesn't say, "Hey, slow down! We'll get you lunch in an hour and a half." No, instead we hear ads like, "If your pizza isn't at your table in five minutes, then your lunch is free." We are conditioned by haste, programmed and trained by internal and external demands.

Not all cultures worship haste. Lunch in Mexico is a delightful, relaxing experience, sometimes followed by a siesta. Lunch in the United States can be a leisurely experience, too—but we have to work at it, and we'd certainly never get anywhere if we dawdled every day. We lead rushed and urgent lives because we buy into our hidden cultural messages.

Another cultural message of haste and urgency is that busier people are worth more as human beings. I once heard the story of a man who bought a fake car phone, just so he could look busy and important at traffic intersections on the way to and from work. Like cars and large homes, busy lives are a status symbol. Our neighbors might wonder about us if we chose simply to sit crosslegged in our yard among the pecans, staring at the autumn leaves falling. We fear they'd think, *What a sinful waste of time.*

All of the messages relayed to us subliminally need to be brought to our conscious mind and fought against in prayer. It's been said many times, but bears repeating: God made us human *beings,* not human *doings.* The feelings associated with urgency—increased heart rate, pumping adrenaline, TMJ, headaches, tight muscles, the tendency to drive too fast, to talk too much, to speed from one activity to another without reflection—rob us of the great pleasures of peace, serenity, and quietude so necessary for an enriched relationship with God.

HOW TO FIGHT URGENCY

I started this chapter on a Wednesday. I woke up that morning with a list of almost twenty things to do that day, including items like getting permission to use a poem, calling a number of people both in and out of town, picking up several items at the grocery store, and stopping at the bank, the bookstore, the post office. I started early; I knew that if I didn't, the hungry ducks on my list would nibble away my whole day. By noon, I had conquered almost half the list, and by five, I was down to four items.

Then a new and terrible insight hit me. I had let my entire day be governed by all the stuff I *had* to do and none of the stuff I *wanted* to do. Not on the list were the following items: prayer, working on this chapter, my Bible study group, family time, and choir—five activities far more meaningful than anything on the list. Yes, I had managed to include these five items during the day, but my focus and attention and energy had been on the by-now smeared and dog-eared piece of paper I had carried with me in my purse since 7:45.

Wrong emphasis.

Like Lily in the opening story, I had compiled the list

the night before, knowing it was going to be a doozy. Feeling swamped by life, I felt better writing the demands down on paper, as if in the act of writing them down, I could tame their hold on my emotions and time. As I tried to get to sleep, combing my memory for any errand I'd mistakenly left off, I felt victimized by the sheer number of events required of me the next day. *I had not chosen most of the things to do on my list. They had chosen me.* I felt that life was hurling a blizzard of errands and duties and requirements at me, and there was nothing I could do except wade through the snow drifts and hope to survive.

Wrong attitude.

By the end of the day, I arrived home from choir and completed one more item on the list, getting a babysitter for the next night. I had knocked off all but three items and should have been able to sink gratefully into bed, exhausted but happy I'd accomplished so much. Instead I noticed a wretched phenomenon. The adrenaline that my body had produced to push me through my list did not stop surging out of my glands. Instead of relaxing, I continued to bounce around the house, looking for domestic things to do—folding the laundry, tidying the kitchen. I had become addicted to my own adrenaline and couldn't shut it off.

Wrong response.

Because I was supposed to be writing this chapter on the idol of urgency, I realized God was trying to tell me something—and I'd better listen!

Here is what I learned as I stumbled through that day, my eyes and ears open prayerfully, in a new way. First, my Bible study and theological reflection group began with a ten-minute musical prayer from Taize, a nondenominational center for Christian renewal in France. The repetition of the words, "Father, let me hear You," and the soft intercessions settled all our scattered and frantic spirits leading us to focus on Jesus and His grace. As I sat on that couch, letting the music soothe me, I remembered how soft Christian tapes used to fill me with prayer and peace, slowing down the rush-hour traffic in my soul. I had forgotten the power of ten minutes spent with quiet music in a place with no telephone. Quiet renditions of old favorite hymns, Gregorian chants, Taize tapes, or music from popular singers like John Michael Talbot—the styles are varied, but the effect is calming. Hint from the Lord: When even our prayer lives begin to resemble a list, the power of music can help get us back in touch with the gentleness and peace of the Holy Spirit.

Next, at the end of the session, several members of the group discussed how refreshed we felt after the Taize tape and wondered why our lives had become tangled knotted skeins of things to do. I did not initiate this discussion. I had simply prayed for something to say in this chapter because this topic so clearly had me by the tail.

Three of my friends offered wonderful insights, giving gifts of wisdom I'd like to pass on here. Anne said that when she faced horrendous list days, she flat-out prayed for time. To her amazement and gratitude, the Lord often honored her prayer—in unexpected ways. For instance, she'd be standing tenth in line at the grocery store with a cart piled high, and suddenly a new check-out stand would open up and the checker would come to her. Or, she would "coincidentally" run into people on her long list of phone calls, thus saving her much time.

God is interested in the texture of our days. One thing I've come to accept is that some days are busier than others; if we choose to participate in life, we cannot avoid this ebb and flow. On the flow days, when urgency drives us and we lurch (late) from one event to the next, we can pray for time like Anne. And God will give us little corners to cut so we don't have to be so breathless. It also helps on the flow days to know that ebb days will return and that if we pray and pare down our schedules, we will not ultimately drown.

Jane offered this insight from a workbook she had once completed on time management. The authors had suggested that, before beginning the course, she make a list of what she would do with more time, if she had it. The authors warned about what I call the nibble phenomenon: If we do not guard our time carefully, surrounding it with a sacred fence, it will be eaten away by the same kind of meaningless activities we try so hard to avoid. We clear our lists only to find that more junky errands have weaseled onto them. My husband, Stockton, says, "Errands expand to fill the time allotted." Jane reminded us of preserving the sacredness of the time we do manage to clear, so that these precious, hard-won, private minutes will not be tinged by the same urgency that drives so much of the rest of our lives.

Angela closed the discussion by teaching us the breath prayer. Taken from Ron DelBene's book entitled *The Breath of Life,* Angela outlined how to pray so that literally every breath we take becomes a prayer—at stop lights, in pressure-filled business meetings, in the carpool line, as well as in our special prayer time.

First, get yourself alone with God. Then, identify the most comfortable way you address God in prayer—Jesus, Christ, Lord, God, Father, whatever is the most familiar way you talk to God. Next, picture Jesus in Mark 10:51, asking the blind beggar, "What do you want me to do for you?" only picture yourself in the beggar's place. Tell Him honestly, in six to nine syllables (syllables, not words). An example of a breath prayer is, "Jesus, guide me in your will," or "Father, lead me into health."[1] Then, taking five minutes at first, simply say the first few syllables of your prayer as you breathe in, and the last few syllables as you breathe out.

We can practice this prayer anywhere, especially when the power of the nonessential begins to goad us into restlessness. As she concluded telling us how to pray this way, Angela included a warning. She said, "Do not, I repeat, do not pray this way unless you want to see some serious changes in your life." She related how she had been standing in a long grocery line (why are grocery lines so stressful?) praying and breathing, when the woman ahead of her—someone she didn't know—turned to her and began to pour out her heart.

The breath prayer is one way we can follow Paul's injunction to pray unceasingly. The breath prayer is also one way we can calm the urgency pushing at us, making us more in tune with God's time and His will for our lives.

URGENCY AS A CHOICE

Seven-year-old Jimmy swings from the Tarzan rope in his back yard, yelling, "Ah ih ah ih ah!" in good jungle form, only he slips off the rope and punctures his rib cage with one of the decorative spikes lining the garden. Mom and Dad rush out, take one look at the blood, load Jimmy's limp form in the car, and break all speed limits getting to the hospital.

This scenario is a true emergency. Urgency is the correct response.

Two days later, Dad gets caught on the freeway behind the collision of a pickup and an eighteen wheeler while he's trying to deliver papers to a client who has threatened to fire his consulting company if he doesn't receive the signed originals by 5:00. The last thing the boss said to Dad was, "Don't mess this one up. We don't get the papers there by 5:00, we're dead meat, especially you." So Dad sits in his stalled car, eyeing the mile-long pileup of vehicles sitting four deep on the expressway. Dad has hated his job for almost two years now, but he especially hates it today. He stabs the radio buttons, flicking quickly from station to station. He runs his fingers through his hair. He has to go to the bathroom. His heart races, and he wishes he could throw the papers out the window, walk home, and move to Montana, where he's always wanted to live.

Dad's body experienced the same symptoms in both scenes, but in the second instance, the sense of urgency was artificial. The company that needed the papers used "Hurry, hurry, hurry" to bully Dad's company in a power play for more control over their performance. Dad's boss passed the threat along to Dad, who hated his job anyway but played along because it is culturally unacceptable to say to one's boss, "Personally, I don't care whether these papers get there at all. I'd rather be fishing in Montana." As a result, Dad experienced urgency and all the debilitating physical wear and tear on his body over something that—unlike Jimmy—he really didn't care about.

As I have studied the problem of worshiping urgency, I've noticed some interesting things. First, we honestly feel that we cannot control the urgent events that happen to us. Sometimes this is true, in the case of Jimmy's accident, for instance. That particular urgent accident was imposed on an otherwise calm Saturday afternoon.

A close examination, however, reveals that much of the

urgency we feel put upon us by bosses, necessity, or life in general we can actually control. We are not the helpless victims our culture tells us we are. We can master and manipulate our own situations, even when we think we're trapped in a heart-pulsing, miserable spot. For example, Jimmy's dad, sitting on the freeway, has several choices. He can continue to twitch and squirm impatiently, riding the conveyor belt straight toward a heart attack by hyperventilating in the hot car. Or, he can turn off the radio and consider his options.

The most dramatic option he has is to quit his job. He could actually walk into his boss's office next week, or next month, or next year and tell him that the rewards from his stressful position do not outweigh the cost in terms of time spent with family or quality of life and that he is making arrangements to do what he's always wanted to do—work a small ranch in Montana.

We are never as trapped as we feel. Sometimes courage and a little foresight are all it takes to slow down the pace of our lives. Sometimes even daydreaming about quitting alleviates stress.

Another option Jimmy's dad has is to keep his job, but to ask for a less demanding client. This particular client was notorious for making him hustle, calling at the last minute and being rude and pushy on the phone. Jimmy's dad has enough seniority to request another client.

A further option is to keep both his job and this particular client but decide to use the time on the interstate to meditate or pray. Instead of punching the radio buttons, catching nerve-jangling snatches of songs, he can find some quiet elevator music, lean back, close his eyes halfway, take deep breaths, and relax. He can pray the breath prayer and accept the things he cannot change.

Jimmy's dad is only as trapped as he allows himself to feel. Urgency is not a given, even in a situation like this. Urgency is a choice.

Stephen Covey, in *The Seven Habits of Highly Effective People*, describes four quadrants of time management: (1) urgent and important; (2) not urgent, but important; (3) urgent, but not important; and (4) not urgent, not important.[2] He says many people live in quadrant 1 by mistake, moving from one crisis to another. We can choose not to live like that.

Another insight into idolatry is that, in spite of our complaints, we must be getting something out of allowing ourselves to be tyrannized by the urgent or we would find a way to stop the behavior. Jimmy's dad may feel important because this is his company's biggest client, and his ego swells a bit every time he is sent out on the expressway to deal with this pushy person. Many times we satisfy our egos when we can answer "Busy" to the question, "How are things going?" For those of us prone to lists, the feeling of accomplishment at the end of the day is rewarding, even if we have trouble going to sleep as a result. We feel worth more because we have pushed to finish a monumental list of things to do, and we have physical evidence of success in the form of a crossed-off piece of paper.

There are other reasons, too. Some of us fear that we might become bored if the urgency should disappear from our lives. Boredom, we suspect, would be far worse than pressure. Busyness equals happiness. Even if we accepted a leisurely pace for ourselves, we fear that others would think we were wasting our lives. We might even turn into crashing bores ourselves, lost at cocktail parties because we have no interesting chitchat about our hectic lives.

Staying trapped in the urgent also keeps our lives at a comfortable shallowness. If Jimmy's dad turned off the urgency, he might have to examine exactly why he has failed to do what he really wanted to do with his life.

Urgency becomes a habit, and habits, as we all know, are hard to break. Sometimes it's easier to say "yes" to the one extra thing that will ruin the peace of our day because we have not sufficiently developed the abililty to say "no." Sometimes the habit of riding the whitewater of urgency is easier than struggling against the current.

Human beings tend to do exactly what we want to do, despite our protestations to the contrary. When I'm tempted to let myself get caught up in a net of urgency, I need to look closely to see what I am getting as a reward. Do I really want peace? Do I really want the self-examination that time alone with God allows? Am I willing to let chores and errands slide so that I can experience a less hectic day? When night comes, which is more important: to feel my own personal accomplishment, or God's tranquillity?

The end of May, the beginning of September, and the entire month of December are predictably busy times when I simply sigh and pray just to get through the days with grace. Though I have some choice as to what events I take on, Things To Do seem to jump on my calendar without my consent and gloat at me. I am aware of these pitfalls in the calendar and can sometimes plan in advance to build in quiet times. Other times, though, life seems to gang up on me unexpectedly, and suddenly I am drowning without warning. Whenever I feel the power of the urgent beginning to tighten my chest, I have to force myself to stop and examine the situation, then ask God to help me slow myself down. Inevitably, sooner or later, this prayer is answered. We simply must want God's pace more than our own.

When Stockton was in seminary, we heard about an experiment done to examine the power of urgency. The experiment went something like this. Advisors informed students of an important meeting with a bigwig who could help them—or hinder them—in getting a job after seminary. Each student was told that promptness was this important person's main virtue and that he was expecting the student in five minutes across campus. Planted along the student's route was a young woman in obvious distress, weeping alone on a bench.

Would the students stop and help her?

Very few did. Most walked on past, compelled by the urgency of the appointment. I wonder how many times I have passed by the opportunity to minister or show love to someone because I've been in a hurry to get somewhere else. This experiment made me stop and think about the purpose of our lives, the spontaneity of ministry, and the utter selfishness of being tied to a list of things to do.

Urgency is a choice. Day by day we choose to worship God or urgency. As the days slide into years, and years into a lifetime, we wonder: Will we find ourselves with unfinished lists left by the bedside, like Lily, or will we find ourselves at peace? A frightening question, but one worth asking.

Chapter 6

SELF-FULFILLMENT

See how we trifle here below, fond of these earthly toys: our souls, how heavily they go, to reach eternal joys.

—ISAAC WATTS

In the seventeenth century, Blaise Pascal, then a sixteen-year-old whiz kid mathematician, wrote a paper envied by Descartes because of its enormous success in Parisian circles. At nineteen, Pascal invented a calculating machine. After a narrow brush with death, he became converted to the inner spiritual life, rejecting fame and worldly success. He decided to write a Christian apology, to defend his faith to his friends still caught up in the glamor of fashionable French life. He took reams of notes and outlined his massive treatise.

Then he died.

In 1937, Amelia Earhart set out with copilot Frederick J. Noonan to fly around the world. Already a record breaker for her transatlantic flights, Amelia waved girlishly at the camera, wearing her leather helmet and ear flaps in a famous picture snapped right before take-off.

Her plane disappeared somewhere between New Guinea and Howland Island.

Last year, a young woman valiantly fought lung and liver cancer, determined to live so she could finish raising her six-year-old son. She died before his next birthday.

What do these three people have in common? They died without completing their dreams. They lurched out of life unfulfilled.

Pascal's Christian masterpiece, *Pensees*—fragmented though it is—remains a religious and philosophical classic even today. The irony of his life is that he suffered from the conflict between God and the world, God and fame, God and self-love. He vacillated between his need for the esteem brought him by his scientific discoveries and writings, and the need to spurn worldly self-fulfillment. His great religious defense remains in fragmented form because he was tempted back into science and math, composing instead the *Elements de geometri,* and publishing his findings on cycloid curves before continuing his Christian work.

Blaise Pascal knew firsthand the tension many of us feel between the desire to fulfill our lives in terms we've defined as successful and the need to give our lives fully to God.

Psychologist Abraham Maslow established a hierarchy of human needs, beginning with the basics like food and shelter, and culminating with self-actualization. In his terms, self-actualization refers to the full use of our individual human potential, capabilities, and talents. Many people have peak experiences of self-actualization, in experiences of happiness and fulfillment. The problem is that our culture has bought into this kind of self-fulfillment as a kind of heaven on earth, to be sought after at all costs. Our accomplishments (we think) are a means to this end.

Maslow's self-actualization includes such qualities as "wholeness, perfection, aliveness, uniqueness, effortlessness, self-sufficiency, . . . beauty, goodness, and truth."[1] Christianity also promises these same qualities, but through a different process. It is through self-emptying that we achieve Christfullness, which in turn gives us back our selves in the most fulfilling way. If we seek accomplishments for themselves or because we think they will make us feel whole, we are on a journey into dust. Paradoxically, if we seek Christ first, we gain ourselves, and our achievements lead toward a higher, holier end.

When I was a preteen, I made a list of all the things I wanted to do before I died. Tops on the list was shaving my legs. Next, I wanted to be asked out on a date by a cute boy. I also wanted a pair of Capezio shoes. I look back and chuckle at that young girl, so limited in her desires. Yet if I made a list now of what I want to do before I die, the items might look as silly to God as my earlier list does to me now.

Jesus cried, "It is finished!" on the cross before He died. I have read many interpretations on what He meant, but I think we all share a yearning not to die until we are completed. It is hard for us to recognize that when we love God first and foremost, we are already complete in Him.

Accomplishments. Self-fulfillment. Completion. All are gifts from God, but can tempt us to commit idolatry, if these gifts are sought for themselves.

ACCOMPLISHMENTS

Accomplishments come in many forms. They are items on a resume: secretary of the Symphony League, vice-president of Texaco, Ph.D. from Harvard, head pastor of Big Church, USA. Seen in a list, or as credentials after a name, such achievements provide proof that we are authentic human beings, respected and admired. They are the world's stamp of approval for our personhood.

We can measure accomplishments in other ways as well. Making lots of money is an accomplishment, especially for someone with no college education or other listable credentials. Being a kingmaker, the unseen power behind the power, is also an achievement in influence, leading toward a more private satisfaction.

Accomplishments come in less measurable ways, too. Raising healthy, functioning children into adulthood is no small accomplishment in these treacherous times. Auditing a class in a new foreign language, learning to play an instrument, overcoming one's shyness in a crowd—all these constitute accomplishments as well.

What one person takes for granted may be an enormous accomplishment for another. For example, my father-in-law, a brilliant federal judge on the Fifth Circuit, fell ill with ideopathic pulmonary fibrosis. Long after the disease would have killed a less-determined person, he forced himself to get out of bed every day—though it sometimes took him almost three hours to bathe and get dressed—and he worked for several hours before reversing the routine and going to bed. He followed this painful practice up until the day he was finally hospitalized, just before his death. This accomplishment of going to work, what many take for granted daily, was one of the most magnificent human endeavors I have ever witnessed.

Accomplishments alone aren't idols. In fact, accomplishments are often acts of stupendous and miraculous faith. Achievements become idols when we start defining ourselves by them—when we believe our own resumes, when we puff ourselves up with pride, when we base our self-esteem on what we've done instead of on the more elusive promise that we are precious children of God.

Like those of many adolescents, my high school years were fraught with insecurity. I had no sense that God loved me, or that I was worth anything other than what I could accomplish. So I set out to prove my worth to myself. I was elected Secretary of the Student Council. I was number one on the tennis team. I became a member of the National Honor Society. I needed these accomplishments to buttress my personhood because I felt like a nonperson, a nonentity, without them. They defined me.

As I have grown in faith and confidence, I have known more and more that my worth is based on the love of God. Nothing I can do will make me special. No awards I can earn will make me a better person. This is not to say that honors and accomplishments are not still a temptation. They are, because I'm a human being living in a competitive society, and because I'm not as spiritually mature as I hope one day to be. However, now the taproot of my being grows in the rich soil of the being of Christ instead of in the shifting sands of worldly accomplishment.

The problem with developing a good resume is that it is a bottomless pit. The ideal person we want to be remains just a few accomplishments short of our vitas. No matter how many poems we publish, how many job offers we receive, we really need more to prove to ourselves—and to others we consider "important"—that we are worthy of respect. Like the shimmering puddle in the middle of the highway, the mirage of self-contentment lies just down the road.

We tend to be pleased with what we've done with our lives until we read someone else's résumé who is our age and has done far more. We are like the self-made millionaire who bought one of the biggest yachts in America. He sailed out into the Caribbean feeling great about himself until, sure enough, one of the biggest yachts in the *world* sailed by. Suddenly, he once again felt like the little poor boy who started out throwing newspapers at the age of seven. All his worldly achievements could not lift him beyond that early self-image. Worldly accomplishments cannot redeem us. They cannot save us from ourselves.

As I have grown older, I have noticed a changing trend in my attitude toward accomplishments. In high school, I *was* my accomplishments. I seemed to have no identity outside the list of things I'd done. In college, something interesting happened. I started to have a good time. I stopped trying to get elected to offices. I stopped studying for grades. The old-style accomplishments became a burden.

However, my needs simply shifted to different arenas. It was important to have lots of dates, and accomplishments took the form of invitations to certain parties. I was defined, again, not for who I was, but for who I went out with and who my friends were.

Same problem, different pasture.

As a young adult, accomplishments took the form of

getting a respectable job, marrying and having children, getting advanced degrees. Then, when I turned forty, accomplishments took a strange turn. My resume fell far short of what I felt it should be at my "advanced" age. After the initial depression over my failed opinion of myself, God gave me a great gift. What I wanted out of life shifted. My goals became inner goals, and what I wanted to accomplish became things like forgiveness for people who'd hurt me in the past, patience, an ability to listen better, to live in the present, to relinquish perfectionism, to remain calm in times of stress.

Aha! I thought. Surely a life directed by the Holy Spirit from within was closer to the kind of résumé God wanted— which was, what? Somehow, I don't think God is impressed with a single item on the conventional résumé I have worked up for job applications. God would probably be most happy if we were able to list anything from Galatians 5:22-23 beside our names. Rather than citing our degrees, honors, and awards, we'd probably make Him happiest by working on love, joy, peace, patience, kindness, goodness, faithfulness, gentleness, and self-control. These fruit of the spirit are a far cry from what the world thinks is important, yet they are much more difficult to accomplish. For instance, getting a Ph.D. is a piece of cake compared to learning to live in gentleness and self-control.

The image of St. Francis comes to mind, standing buck naked in the town square, having relinquished all his worldly possession. When all is said and done, we stand like that before God, stripped of all the protective devices with which we shield our nakedness—our possessions, our relationships, our accomplishments.

The great freedom Jesus gives us is to be ourselves, defined by His love and our inner qualities and gifts rather than by any kind of show we put on for the world. We are freed, like uncaged birds, because God loves us unconditionally—without degrees, promotions, elected offices, or a cool crowd surrounding us.

In a speech delivered at Virginia Seminary recently, the Archbishop of Canterbury, George Carey, made an interesting observation about the movie *Mr. Holland's Opus.* In the movie, Richard Dreyfuss spends much of his life focused on accomplishing his great musical masterpiece, the work that will bring him fame and admiration. Yet over the years, his love for his students absorbed his energies. True accomplishment for Mr. Holland came when, after the orchestra played his "masterpiece," one of his students said, "Mr. Holland, we are your opus." Mr. Holland had sacrificed the idol of personal achievement for love for others.

Christian writer Henri Nouwen, in an interview with *The Wittenberg Door,* once commented on the real suffering he saw in our country. "There are so many Americans who are so lonely, so isolated, and so guilt-ridden and they are choosing the adulation of the world as a means of coping."[2] Worldly adulation of our accomplishments makes us emptier, not fuller. Yet we are hoodwinked, again and again, trying to fill ourselves up with unnutritious stuff.

Worshiping our accomplishments goes hand in hand with another idol, the god of self-reliance, one of this culture's major deities. We hate dependence. We love the exhilaration of knowing we "did it our way." We look at our accomplishments and think, "I earned that award," or "I really paid for that one." Seldom do we look over our resumes and think, "I'm alive by the grace of God, and it's only by the same grace that my fingers work well enough to type out this list of accomplishments, much less achieve them in the first place." Humility is the proper lens through which we see what we've done. But humility isn't as much fun or, well, as self-satisfying as relying on ourselves.

Which brings us to the next topic.

SELF-FULFILLMENT

I once attended a ceremony in a great granite hall in honor of a political figure. As "The Star Spangled Banner" echoed off the slick, polished rock walls and floors, I looked out over the sea of expensive suits and coiffed hair and thought, How gratifying to end a worthy career in the presence of the former president's wife, the governor, and so many other national and state dignitaries.

How few of us get the flowers before we die. Most of us will have to be satisfied with a homily or testimonials at our funerals, which might be enormously gratifying, except that it will be too late for us to enjoy the accolades. Laid out in a box, we will then be deaf to any praise the world has to give.

Ever since our fall in the Garden of Eden, we need "attaboys" and "attagirls" to feel okay about ourselves. Like hungry people, we feed on the praise of others so we can feel full, satisfied. The only problem is that, like real stomach hunger, sooner or later the full, happy feeling goes away, and we are famished again, scrounging around for self-fulfillment in our jobs, in our relationships, and among the comments of our friends.

Nothing illustrates this paradoxical phenomenon like the psychology of success. I have personally known people who have achieved major goals, prodded for many years by the expectation that at last they will be satisfied, joy filled, whole, only to reach the goal and suffer instead from a major depression. When we look to the wrong thing for happiness, its absence is all the more acute.

True self-fulfillment is actually attained by emptying ourselves of ourselves, not by padding ourselves with the success of our plans. However, the process of self-emptying is difficult and complicated because first we have to have a self to give to God. In psychological terms, we need a healthy ego. We need to feel comfortable with who we are, with the person God is sculpting, molding, creating day by day.

Bob had been raised in an alcoholic home. Not only did his sense of self-worth rest on the rock bottom of an empty pond, but he never formed a clear idea of who he was. Like a chameleon, he took on the characteristics of any strong personality he was with. His mother had pushed him toward the priesthood, but his drunken father had beat him physically when he expressed a desire to become anything other than a coach.

When Bob announced his plans to major in education, his father fell on the porch steps in his rage, screaming at Bob, "You'll never amount to anything!"

Through the influence of his girlfriend (later his wife), Bob ended up as the director of Christian education at a large church in the South. The problem was that he couldn't take praise and he couldn't take criticism, and he gave in to every suggestion anyone posed. Who was Bob? He himself didn't know. Until he finally went into counseling, he lived a life of quiet desperation, terrified of offending people, and ineffective in his position.

God had given Bob unique gifts and talents. He gave him a self, a being. Until Bob accepted himself, allowing himself to be "selfish"—to be a real person, to let his self develop into a separate entity—Bob had no real personhood he could give to anyone, much less God. For a number of years, Bob struggled against his mother's constant admonition, "Don't be selfish, don't be selfish," finally realizing that it wasn't selfish to be the person God wants you to be.

When Bob finally differentiated his personhood into a self, then and only then, did he stop trying to fill himself up with others' praise and definitions of who he should be. He said, "Okay, Lord. Here is who I am. I give this person to You." His desperate craving for self-fulfillment eased.

Another variation to the problem of self-fulfillment is the need—and the willingness—to put ourselves on hold while we work toward filling the needs of others. A strong sense of self is necessary to sacrifice our needs for others. We simply cannot do it if our own needs are too great.

Marlene's story is typical in many ways of the struggle of women (and men) in an age of self-fulfillment. Marlene had been raised to marry and have a family. Her mother said, "When you go to college, be sure to get your teaching certificate just in case you ever have to work." In her mother's eyes, "having to work" was a disaster created by the collapse of Plan A—finding a husband.

Her junior year, Marlene almost got engaged to a pre-med student, but something made her break it off. She couldn't shake the niggling feeling that her relentlessly driven fiancé-to-be never really considered her to be a person in her own right but rather saw her as an extension of himself. Marlene reclaimed herself before she tossed her personhood to the care of someone who'd abuse it.

Several years later, after she had taught math and discovered (to her amazement and her mother's chagrin) that she loved teaching, she met Bert, a computer professor at the university where Marlene had started to work on her master's degree. When they were first married, Bert encouraged Marlene to pursue her degree. Then they moved because her husband became head of the computer department at the state university. Suddenly, Marlene found herself in a strange town, friendless, and feeling increasingly isolated by what she jokingly tried to laugh off as her "natural disaster," the birth of triplets.

Drowning at home alone in formula, diapers, and wailing infants, Marlene felt utterly unfulfilled. She missed teaching. She regretted abandoning her degree. She missed adult conversation. With three babies to care for, she never felt as though she had enough time alone with any one of them. She felt too exhausted and emotionally ragged to make friends in the new town.

Fortunately, Marlene had a strong sense of self. Daily (every hour, it seemed, every minute, sometimes every second) she prayed for the strength to get through these early difficult years. Bert helped her when he could and encouraged her. Marlene was temporarily willing to sacrifice her own needs for self-fulfillment, postponing her personal agenda until the triplets entered kindergarten. Then she went back to school, finished her degree, and began teaching again when the kids started first grade.

Our culture tells us to get our needs met at all costs. Don't let anyone stand in your way. Don't let anything, especially something as common and irritating as children, break your stride. This is not merely a women's issue. Dads, too, face the culture's demand for vocational fulfillment on the one hand versus time spent with the family on the other. Many men have had to choose between getting in a respectable sixty billable hours weekly at the law firm and the eager eyes of a daughter who offers a quarter if he'll play with her for just five minutes before work.

Child-rearing is in a national crisis. If we fall for the line that our jobs or our volunteer work is where we must get our strokes, then we will miss the fulfillment of watching our children thrive from the love and attention we've sacrificed to give them. Even if tragedy strikes our children, or they do not turn out as we expect, if we have given them ourselves and our time, we can let God have the results, knowing we've done what we could.

Fortunately, life is a smorgasbord of creative solutions for women and men who want personal job satisfaction and the satisfaction of raising children. Cooperative parenting involving both mom and dad, part-time jobs, or even role reversal gives everyone a chance to thrive. One of the most successful parenting pairs I know includes my sister-in-law, a lawyer who gave up her partnership in a major law firm for a more flexible "of counsel" position, and her husband, a consultant who works out of their home. We do not have to eclipse our own personhood for our children; in fact, to do so is not healthy. The parent who continually martyrs his or her own needs "for the good of the children" is liable to promote guilt and low self-esteem in the child. The same is true for the spouse who becomes a martyr to the other's needs. A temporary sacrifice or postponement of self-fulfillment is not the same as being squelched.

The bottom line in juggling parenthood and job satisfaction is to remember where, ultimately, our selfhood needs are met—in Jesus Christ. As long as we keep our hearts and desires focused on Him, He will lead us into fulfillment. He will pour a lasting satisfaction into our hearts, the kind of refreshment the world cannot give.

Another wrinkle in the discussion of self-fulfillment is discipline. Like good parenting—which takes practice, effort in the face of apparent failure, willingness to try new techniques, and repetition of words and gestures of love— the development of our spiritual personhood takes discipline. Concert pianists often go years without the rewards of soaring success. Struggling to reach small plateau after small plateau, the pianist recognizes that the early rewards and the fulfillment must come from a particular fingering mastered, or the hoped-for crystal-ringing clarity of a phrase, or even the acknowledgment of simply having practiced for the allotted time with no thrills at all.

Our self-fulfillment grows with discipline, too: the discipline of prayer, of love practiced on those who don't seem to notice, of doing our spiritual chores, of going to church, of reading the Bible, of repeatedly seeking the One who feeds us with the bread and water of life. The Samaritan woman at the well understood how Jesus fills us up. Hungry for self-worth, she had lived with five different men trying to be satisfied. Well water, like self-fulfillment in the natural world, leaves us thirsting for more; but the water Jesus gives us to drink fills us completely, so we no longer thirst for our egos' needs to be met by our circumstances.

However, being human, we don't often live in the state of spiritual satiety, the pleasant lull after a gourmet lunch. Getting through the day, swatting the swarms of buzzing, conflicting demands on our time, on our needs, on our dreams, often leaves us feeling dissatisfied spiritually. Oddly enough, though, sometimes those times of being scattered, frustrated, lost, or unfulfilled turn out, in retrospect (of course) to be times of the greatest fulfillment. On a bad day, the concert pianist misses notes and creates discord, but he knows that by the time of the concert, discipline will win out, and most likely, the cacophony will turn into harmony.

Self-fulfillment is similar to happiness. Sought after as a goal, it eludes us like a butterfly. But if we are busy with the tasks Jesus has put in our paths, then self-fulfillment wings its way into the clearing of our lives, fluttering and lighting gently on our shoulder.

COMPLETION

I love the cycles of life. Not just the summer-winter cycles, or the other natural rhythms built into our days, but the way life seems to come back around where we started, with fuller understanding. As my friend and editor Alyse Lounsberry once said to me, it's as though we circle the mountain again and again, each pass increasing our wisdom as we near the top.

My husband, Stockton, tells of one such circle. He graduated from law school and went to work in Austin, Texas, for a law firm based in Midland. From Austin, he traveled to Midland several times, working with both Austin and Midland colleagues until he left the law practice to enter seminary. Returning to Texas from Virginia Seminary, he went first to Waco, then to Houston, and was recently called, of all places, to Midland, where some of his former colleagues go to our church, Holy Trinity. This part of his journey came full cycle when he performed a funeral for one of the law firm's widows, and out in the congregation he saw almost all the members of the old firm. This time around, though, he knew many of them on a spiritual basis.

Two of the most meaningful years of my childhood were spent in Richmond, Indiana, among the Quakers. In sixth grade, my best friend and I walked to school every day discussing animatedly the novels we had each read, *Jane Eyre, The Chestry Oak, Daddy Long Legs, The Little Princess, The Secret Garden.* Years later, I returned to Richmond, where I sought out my friend and we walked up the same street, discussing *Crime and Punishment* in a critique as lively and earnest as those we had as children. We had come full circle around the mountain.

In an ideal world, our lives would not end until we had come full circle, until our jobs on earth had been finished, until we had a chance to say good-bye, until we had tied up all the loose ends, until we were satisfied knowing we were complete. Instead, we often die interrupted, our lives broken by circumstance, sadness, guilt; and we leave things undone, unsaid, wondering why we were put on the earth in the first place.

Literature gives us many examples of gruesome, miserable, tragic deaths. Hamlet, for example, struggles throughout the whole play against killing his uncle to avenge his father's death, hemming, hawing, stalling around for four-and-a-half long acts. When he finally gets around to stabbing the king, his procrastination causes the deaths of most of the rest of the cast, including himself.

Less bloody, but more frighteningly close to home, is American writer Theodore Dreiser's novel *Sister Carrie*, an example of American naturalism. In the first half of the book, Carrie runs off to New York with a wealthy Chicago banker. The second half of the book details the banker's slow slide into poverty and oblivion. He finally dies an unknown bum on Skid Row—the kind of meaningless, scary death dreaded by most of us.

The closest example in literature to an ideal death is portrayed in another American writer's book, *Death Comes for the Archbishop,* by Willa Cather. A French priest named Latour comes to New Mexico as a missionary. Against many adversities, he spends his life building a cathedral in the wilderness. Instead of returning to France, he chooses to die among the people he loves, lying in state in his great monument to Jesus while the bells toll and the people flock in droves to pay him homage. What a way to go! A long life lived to the honor of Jesus Christ, finished off at a ripe old age in heavenly and earthly glory and surrounded by an entire countryside of people who love and revere you.

Life, like literature, reveals death in less fulfilling terms. Death truncates lives, whisking friends and relatives away before we are ready. Those left behind face the clumsy task of raveling together the strands of our loved ones' lives, though we incompletely understand their unfinished dreams.

The good news is that even if we die in a car wreck this very afternoon on the way to the hardware store, we are complete in ways we don't understand. God's agenda is not our agenda; and while we think we have particular goals to reach, these aspirations exist in only one part of time, the part we can understand. We need to be reminded that chronology is only one dimension of a magnificent concept we cannot fully comprehend. God operates without a calendar, without a watch. Time on earth is experienced linearly, while God's time—well, I certainly can't say for sure how it's experienced, except I've had moments of joyous spiritual exhilaration when time as we know it seemed not to exist at all.

For all we know, the short life of a baby who dies in its first month on earth has as much meaning to God as the long life of a Christian philanthropist. God simply doesn't measure anything the way we do. We cannot forget we live in the crosshairs of two dimensions, one of which we understand imperfectly. Put another way, Christians dance to two contrapuntal tunes, one temporal and one eternal; and though the one song may stop abruptly before we think it should, the other tune continues, and it lifts us into eternity on its never-ending melody.

As we dance through our days here on earth, we must remember to listen for the other song.

The biblical example we are given is Jesus. His three-year ministry must have seemed unfinished to his disciples; cruel circumstances seemed to have cut Him down prematurely. In the Garden of Gethsemane, Jesus prayed to avoid death, much as we would. Maybe He didn't want to suffer. Or perhaps, trapped as a human in chronological time as we are, He could not yet fully grasp God's time and the resurrection in the same way He would understand it on Easter morning.

I don't know. Yet, this is the example of completion we are given, not an elderly, successful evangelist, surrounded on his painless deathbed by doting family and friends. No, in fact,

Jesus' example is exactly the opposite in every regard—a life cut short, an excruciating death suffered alone. Yet we cannot forget His last words: "It is finished." He had accomplished what He'd been sent to earth to do.

The young woman mentioned earlier, who died in spite of her resolve, leaving behind a six-year-old son, also left behind her husband whose mother had died when he, too, was young. As he struggles now to raise their son, this man has come full cycle, but this time filled with wisdom and love. Strains of another, sweeter melody mingle through the gloomy notes of grief.

Accomplishments. Self-fulfillment. Completion. All are met in Jesus. In fact, all our needs, especially the need to prove our goodness, are met through Him.

Chapter 7

GOODNESS

There was a little girl who had a little curl
Right in the middle of her forehead;
When she was good, she was very, very good,
And when she was bad she was horrid.

              —MOTHER GOOSE

Little Lisa scrambled over the rock pile, laughing in the gurgly, deep-throated way delighted children laugh. Like a goat, she scuttled around the limestone obstacles, well ahead of her pursuer, Becky Smith, whose wild red hair bobbed up and down as she panted, giggling, after Lisa.

Suddenly, Lisa's shoelace caught on a jagged edge and down she went, scraping both of her knobby, freckled knees and cutting her face on a sharp rock. Becky started to cry when she saw Lisa. Lisa looked like a bloody monster. Dark red drops had dribbled onto the front of her new ruffled blouse, and her frightened hand movements quickly smeared more blood all over her cheeks and chin and hands and hair. At first too stunned to cry, Lisa, too, began to wail when she saw her own blood.

Out planting geraniums in the yard next door, Lisa's mother tripped twice getting to her daughter. When she discerned that the wound was superficial, she knelt down and held the child close to her. In her terror, Lisa soaked up her mother's quiet affection, finally calming down as her mother patted her, stroking her hair and cheek. Lisa loved her mother fiercely and never seemed to get enough close hugs. Because her mother was very strict about socially correct behavior, Lisa never felt she measured up. She hung on whimpering just a little longer for the attention.

Then a thought, sharper than the rock, tore her five-year-old conscience: If my mother knew that I picked my nose in public, she would never love me this much. The child started crying again, this time from sadness because she couldn't tell her mother the truth.

I heard this story from a grown woman. She recounted that particular moment as the first stepping stone in her journey into the stream of self-awareness. At age five, she knew in specific, nonnegotiable terms, I am not good. I am constantly tempted to break a rule very, very important to my mother. The corollary to this realization,

I am therefore not worth my mother's love, broke her small heart.

Though picking our noses is hardly the criterion for human badness, to this sensitive five year old, picking her nose represented one of the worst behaviors she knew—besides, of course, picking on her little brother. But sometimes he deserved it, so teasing him wasn't as bad in her mind.

This story encapsulates the human dilemma. At age five, age twenty, age eighty, most of us do something against our code of ethics and realize that we are not innately, automatically good. Try as we might, we cannot keep all the rules. We may be able to fool the people around us, but sooner or later, if we are honest human beings, we can no longer fool ourselves.

Worse, as we mature, the rules get more complicated and more vague. Five year olds are considered good if they share their toys, mind their parents, don't pinch, don't whine, and use tissues. For adults, goodness is more elusive. Was I truly good for baking the casserole for Mrs. Jones, when I secretly hope that she'll nominate me for an office I want in the ladies club? Was I truly good to sell my house to that young couple at an advertised "bargain" price, suspecting that the air conditioning was about to blow?

If I look closely at my life, I begin to notice an unattractive trend. In the back yard of my personality, I have a well of pristine water. I also have a septic tank. Unfortunately, much of my behavior comes from both sources because the septic tank leaks into the well. Therefore, as hard as I try, the water I draw isn't pure. My behavior is tainted with mixed motives.

GOODNESS IN THE BIBLE

In Genesis, God created everything, from the crystal blue sky to eggplants, and proclaimed it all good. Even us. Male and female. Because it is God who shapes us in our mother's womb, combining DNA from a selected man and woman into a unique, special blend, we must not forget that we have the capacity for great good. Our potential goodness is a gift along with our very lives. We were created good.

However, after the "apple" incident, we also developed the potential for the opposite. We now have a choice in every circumstance of our lives. As human beings, we walk through our days faced with a myriad of selections for good or evil—whether or not to cheat on our income taxes, whether or not to sneak a drink of alcohol as the designated driver, whether to walk past that mean old witch Madge without speaking or trying to break down the ill will with a greeting.

As Christians, of course, we are exhorted by Jesus and by Paul to choose good. Whether we want to or not, we need to try to mend fences with mean old Madge. Others will know us as Christians by our good works, and not just the good works that are easy and fun, like giving children toys at Christmas. As difficult as the commandment is, we are called to do good to the people who hate us (Matt. 5:44 KJV). The Revised Standard Version translates this into loving our enemies. These good works cost. These good works test our mettle. The most dramatic example I've ever heard of this kind of good deed was the young woman who told the man who attacked her with a knife in the parking lot, "I will pray for you."

The New Testament makes a clear distinction between "good" as an adjective and "goodness" as an innate human quality. The New Testament writers packed the gospels and epistles with good deeds, good works, good reports, good fruit, good will, good conscience, good pleasure, good gifts, good cheer. Only once or twice—for example, Barnabas in Acts 11:24—is a person referred to as "good." In fact, this business of human goodness is a touchy issue. In all three synoptic gospels, Jesus is hailed as "Good Teacher," and He responds, "Why do you call me good? No one is good but God alone" (Luke 18:19).

Taking our cue from the New Testament, we need to be careful and watch how we describe ourselves. We are encouraged to do "good works," but to proclaim ourselves as "good" is idolatry.

Paul wrestles with the dilemma of trying to do good, and failing. I picture Paul as a wiry man with a wrestler's build, often wound up with his own natural energy. I can just see him pacing as he dictates the letter to the people in Rome, circling a dirt floor in his tent at Corinth or in someone's guest room as his argument, too, circles around a central truth of human existence:

> For I do not do what I want, but I do the very thing I hate. . . . For I know that nothing good dwells within me, that is, in my flesh. I can will what is right, but I cannot do it. For I do not do the good I want, but the evil I do not want is what I do. (Rom. 7:15–19)

The problem is sin. We are capable of doing great good, yet we often end up doing evil. No matter how much we want to be "good," we cannot bring ourselves to do good on command. And we certainly cannot bring ourselves to *be* good on command.

Dale Hanson Bourke, in her book *Turn Toward the Wind*, discusses Satan's great lie, coaxing us each day into believing that we don't need God to become good. "'You can change. I believe in you,' the devil says. "Work hard enough, try often enough, plan extensively enough, and you can change yourself.'"[1] We cannot, try though we might.

Fortunately, in Christ, we are both saved from our dilemma and forgiven for trying to do it ourselves. Before Jesus died for our sins, the Jewish law was in effect—a hopelessly difficult and entangled mass of rules that only a few, such as the Pharisees, even attempted to follow. The law told us what was right and wrong, in case our natural senses failed to inform us. Jesus' death and resurrection actually simplified life greatly for those aspiring to do good works, reducing all those scrolls full of rules to two basic commandments.

But there is a catch. We have to recognize our true state of existence, a tension between good and bad. We are called to bring all parts of ourselves to the light. Even when we aspire to love God, our neighbors, and ourselves, we fall short. Even when we want to, we can't always be good. "When we peel away the layers of our false innocence, feigned goodness, and noble intentions, we begin to get at the real foundations of our motives."[2] We must then be willing to accept forgiveness. This is a considerably more humble position than the Pharisees' insistence on self-determined righteousness.

LIVING NO-FAULT LIVES

I could be mistaken, but I don't believe that bad things simply fall from the sky like Bartholomew's oobleck in Dr. Seuss's story. I don't agree with the bumper sticker announcing that bad stuff just happens. Seems to me that bad things happen as a direct result of error, accident, poor judgment, evil choices, or natural forces. Some bad things happen because of other people's bad choices, not our own, so it seems as though we are skipping along our merry way and get splattered by something unattractive out of the blue sky.

The problem I have with the bumper sticker is that it reflects a current trend in our country: to disclaim any share in the problems plaguing humankind since the Fall.

"It's not my fault." Sometimes this statement is true. Sometimes it isn't our fault. To live by this creed alone, though—to be unwilling to examine our part in an unfortunate affair—is one way we worship goodness instead of God. We all want to wash our hands of sticky problems. Like Pilate, we don't want a stain on our reputation. We're clean. We're untouched. It's not our fault. It's not our problem. What was Adam's response when he got into trouble with God over the apple? "It's not my fault. Talk to Eve." And what was Eve's response? "It's not my fault. That sneaky snake made me do it." As my friend Angela says, believing Satan's lie that we can/should be good necessitates a second lie: since we are not good and we have already eaten the apple, in order to cover ourselves, we point the finger. "Somebody else made me do it." Jesus' disclaimer that only God is good is critically important.

Children stand next to the cookie jar covered with crumbs, their large, innocent eyes beseeching us to believe, first, that they didn't eat the cookies; then, when that doesn't wash, they try to convince us that it wasn't their fault because they never would have done it if little sister Patricia hadn't told them to. We are very much like those children, only more sophisticated in our methods of delusion.

The current culture encourages this kind of duplicity. For example, it's an age of no-contest, no-fault divorce. Used to be that if a marriage fell apart, at least one, if not two adults stood responsible. Not these days. Now it's possible to walk away, smug and happy, free at last, and I'm not responsible! It's not my fault! I am still good, in my own eyes and in the eyes of the law.

The only problem is that most children of divorced parents seem to have difficulty accepting the situation. Also, feelings and regrets haunt us: Maybe if I'd listened to him more (even though he was a jerk) . . . maybe if I'd have let her refinish the den (even if I hated the new decor) instead of squelching the project . . . maybe if we'd gone to counseling . . . maybe . . . maybe we'd still be together.

If I'm so innocent, why don't I feel clean? Why don't I feel as good as I supposedly am?

Another part of the sickness of our culture is our collective need to be good, to ascribe innocence where we should admit guilt. This truth intersected our lives in a deeply painful way. Four years ago in March, two young boys high on homemade speed entered the home of my elderly aunt and uncle in Kerrville, Texas, to rob them. These two teenagers had cased the house for two weeks. When Uncle Clayton put up a fight, the boys beat him and Juliana over the head with a tire iron and a cedar post then stabbed them in the throat eight or nine times to make sure they were dead. Unfortunately, my cousin Adrienne was also living there, eating supper at the time. She, too, was killed.

This crime was unquestionably a violent, premeditated act. The boys admitted it when they were finally caught.

One of them received the death penalty. The other one, the mastermind, did not. One of the most excruciating parts of an already excruciating experience was the trial of the one who got off with life. My family sat on those hard benches in the courtroom in Junction, Texas, and listened to the teamwork of the defense lawyer and a psychiatrist take away every shred of responsibility from the defendant—the poor young man had been abused as a child. So was his sister, though, who instead of living a life of crime had chosen to marry a responsible man and raise a family. When the matter of choice was implied—clearly his sister had taken a different path—the defense attorney took out huge colored charts and pointed to the statistics. The lawyer presented the murderer as an unfortunate victim of life, using statistics to prove that abused males can't help but fall into a life of crime. In addition, he claimed that this "totally helpless" victim was clinically depressed and should have been on medication.

The jury believed that all of the killer's problems were not his fault, and they let him off with life with possible parole in forty years.

I had a great deal of difficulty in forgiving both the killers and the people involved in the trial and have not yet completely come to terms with this tragedy. After several years now, I still have residual grief, not only for my family, but over a court system that loses sight of who the real victims are.

Yet the longer I reflect on the trial, the more I see that, ironically, the system also robbed the young killer. He walked away apparently faultless, innocent of planning a robbery, innocent of drug involvement, innocent of killing three people "for the thrill of it," as he later testified. The lawyer and psychiatrist took away his right to his choices and his responsibility.

They also took away his reasons to repent for what he had done. The most important thing the lawyer and the psychiatrist may have taken away was the killer's chance for the kingdom of heaven. If we are not sorry for what we have done, we cannot repent. If we do not repent, we do not receive everlasting life. Or forgiveness. We are stuck forever dragging along towsacks filled with rocks of guilt.

One of the great gifts of faith is the true goodness, the cleansing we feel, after we've admitted our faults and our sins. If we deny we do bad things, we suffer internally. If we confess those things to God, then we substitute the lesser "good" of maintaining our reputations to the true good that God gives us in our natures, as we were created before the Fall.

HANGING ON TO GUILT

We worship our own goodness when we refuse to admit we've done something wrong and we can't let go of the image of ourselves as good people. On the other side of this problem is the tendency to hang on to guilt, which is really the same problem in reverse. We are so offended by what we have done—we want so much to be perfect—that we torture ourselves with the bad deed over and over and over.

Sarah Jane pushed her dolly stroller over the hump in the throw rug. The wheels stuck. She pushed harder, determined that Baby Susie should get over the hump. Finally, Sarah Jane lunged with the stroller, clearing the hump and crashing into the hall table. Her mother's favorite vase splintered on the tile floor.

Abandoning Baby Susie, Sarah Jane gathered the pieces and ran crying to her mother. "I'm so sorry," she sobbed.

Her mother sighed and took the fragments from Sarah Jane's pudgy little fingers so she wouldn't cut her hands. "It's all right, Sarah Jane." She bent down and hugged her daughter, looking in the teary eyes. "You are more important than the vase." Her mother gingerly took the broken pieces and threw them in the trash underneath the kitchen sink.

The next day, Sarah Jane was drawn to the trash can. She opened the cabinet door and dug around among the orange peels and sandwich crusts until she found the broken vase. She arrayed the pieces in front of her on the kitchen tile, then started to cry again, this time louder and harder the more she thought about what she'd done. As before, she carried the broken pieces to her mother. "I'm so sorry," she repeated through her tears.

This time her mother shut off the vacuum and addressed her daughter firmly. "I have already forgiven you." She cupped Sarah Jane's chin in her hand and looked her straight in the eye. "I want you to understand you are not to go digging around in the wastebasket again for those pieces. I love you. You are free of this."

Like Sarah Jane, we all break vases, and relationships. We shatter each other—intentionally or unintentionally—by our greed, by our selfish desires, by our willfulness. Once we realize what we've done, the knowledge often devastates us. Not only have we hurt someone we love, but we have damaged our own opinion of ourselves. We have done what we've always considered unforgivable.

In true southern gothic form, Hazel Motes is a bizarre character in Flannery O'Connor's novella *Wise Blood.* Gunning his rat-colored car, Hazel runs down and kills another character. In a twisted attempt at expiation, he wears glass shards in his shoes and wraps his chest with barbed wire. Though most of us don't go that far, still, what we do to ourselves emotionally is comparable. The good news here is not just good news, it is excellent news. Jesus does not expect that kind of payment for what we've done wrong. He has already suffered the torture for the worst we can possibly do. All we have to do is to confess, accept His love, and let go.

Like Sarah Jane, though, sometimes we rummage through the trash cans of our lives and pull out the memories of our badness. We flagellate ourselves with how unforgivable we are. Just this weekend, I suffered for several hours over something I had done. Crying into my pillow, I finally pulled my face out, eyes puffy and nose running, and said to my husband, Stockton, "God certainly has a keen sense of irony here. I've just finished writing about this little girl named Sarah Jane, and I can't stop digging through my own trash can. I can't even follow my own advice. What's the matter with me?"

Stockton replied with kindness and perception. "It's okay, honey. Sometimes you can't let go instantly, even when you know you need to. Go ahead. Work through it."

He was right. The next day I woke up knowing God had forgiven me, and I felt very grateful not to be breaking my back with the boulder in my towsack. Sometimes it takes a weekend, sometimes a year, sometimes a lifetime to relinquish our guilt, but when we finally accept God's ac-ceptance of us and give up our self-images of perfect good-ness, we are flooded with relief.

KEEPING THE RULES

Keeping the rules is my favorite method of tricking myself into thinking I'm a good person. Born the first child in a dysfunctional family, I developed exceptional radar for rules. Survival meant quickly comprehending what was accept-able and what was not, and quickly conforming to praiseworthy behavior. By age two, I knew the house rules by heart. The first week of first grade, I internalized both the classroom and the playground rules. When doubt about my motives crept in, I could always console myself with the knowledge that I did not steal the other kids' erasers, I did not say that unkind thing to Janet, and I did not look on James's paper during the test.

The only problem was the slip-ups: when I peeked just a little during the voting for Best Citizen, when I kicked that younger kid accidently-on-purpose, when I did say that unkind thing to Janet because she was mean to me first. These bad deeds were a problem. I couldn't forget them. I couldn't pretend that I didn't do them—I felt too bad. So, since I couldn't erase these black marks, I put them far on the other side of my gigantic score sheet, taking consolation that the check marks for good behavior greatly overshadowed the others.

As I grew older, however, somewhere along the line the correlation between impulse and deed became skewed. I tried to do a friend a favor, and ended up hurting the friend's feelings. Conversely, in another incident, I was rewarded publicly for a job I despised. What I felt bad about inside looked like something good to other people. Like Paul, when I tried to do good, I didn't; and sometimes my bad intentions were unexplainedly redeemed.

Before I could solve this enigma, other questions began to bother me. For instance, was it hypocritical to be nice to someone you didn't like, or was it Christian love? And what about mixed motives? Was anything I ever did pure, or was there always a little prize in it for me? Using the checklist as a means for measuring good behavior was one thing, but this internal stuff was getting too complicated, and too slippery.

It was bad enough when good behavior turned out bad, and bad motives produced good results. But then I started doubting what was "good" in the first place. Was good behavior simply socially and politically appropriate behavior? Philip Hallie points out, "The word good sometimes carries with it connotations of vapidity. Good children, like good examples, fit neatly and quietly and passively into the patterns others have laid down upon them."[3] Is goodness simply passivity? When did the "good" deed that backfired stop being good and start being destructive? Was "good" only in the eye of the beholder? Did you get credit for being good if you just thought nice thoughts and didn't ever interact with people at all? Wasn't every single human exchange, after all, fraught with the potential for misunderstanding and thus the mixing up of good and bad? Help! What was a good deed in the first place?

The problem of goodness had turned into a sinkhole of quicksand. I knew I could never be good, and I wanted the checklist back—a measurable record of good behavior so I could think well of myself when I surveyed and counted all the things I did right.

With this insight into the impossibility of my own goodness, I also realized that Christ had died not just for my blatant sins, but for the subtle ones as well: for all my mixed motives, for the acts of kindness that wound others inadvertently, for self-doubt, for the desire to think well of myself. Christ redeems me every time I open my mouth, and He redeems every gesture I make toward goodness—or evil.

Once I accept that I am not a good person in my own right, no matter how hard I try, then the paradox becomes true: I am good after all because God made me and Christ redeemed me. Like the song says, I am clean because I have been washed in the blood of the Lamb of God. All those years of trying to earn goodness I had missed the point. Goodness is a gift, like life itself.

The hard part is to get my own needs and desires out of the way and keep my eyes focused on Jesus.

ONE LAST DANGER

I have come to accept most of my actions as stemming from dual motives. For instance, I sing in the choir because I want to. I love the choir's camaraderie and the choir members' wonderful sense of humor. The music we sing and the words inspire me, and I always leave choir practice uplifted. I do not have a great voice, but I get pats on the back for being a nice, traditional clergy wife by singing in the choir. Most of my reasons for singing in the choir are therefore quite selfish.

Blessedly, God honors this obligation and turns what is essentially a personally gratifying experience into a means of worship. Self-interest, thus, changes into something good when it is placed on the altar of faith.

As we mature in the faith, our good acts become more spontaneous and selfless. This is the goal. In typical human form, though, sometimes we also focus too much upon the goodness of the deed we have just accomplished. I remember once several years ago spontaneously giving food to a beggar, then actually thinking how nice that was of me. Maybe I'm not such a bad Christian after all.

There goes the good deed, sinking deep in the pond of pride.

The Bible tells us not to hide our lights under a bushel, to show forth our good works so that we might glorify our Father in heaven. The trick is to do our good works with gratitude, not pride; otherwise, we worship the work and our part in it instead of God. God gets hidden under the bushel, even though our good work may have gotten lots of attention. Sigh. As a different bumper sticker says, "Christians are not perfect, just forgiven."

Preoccupation with our own goodness is like rancid perfume. But when we act and live in the Lord's will unconsciously, and praise Him (not ourselves) through our works, our goodness is a fresh scent, attracting others to the Source.

PETER AND JOHN

A glance at John the beloved disciple and Peter the Rock on whom Jesus founded the church sheds some interesting light. At one point, John and his brother missed the point when their mother asked Jesus if her boys could sit at His right hand in the kingdom of heaven. The rest of the time, though, John was the "good" disciple. He was the only one who stayed with Jesus at the cross. He was the obviously responsible one to whom Jesus entrusted the care of His mother. Jesus selected him (along with Peter and James) to witness the transfiguration, and he didn't ask any obtuse questions or make out-of-line comments during the event. Using almost any definition of "good," John was the best of the twelve.

Peter, on the other hand, was a mess. Peter's faith faltered halfway out on the lake, and he sank like a rock. Jesus continually rebuked Peter for missing the point. "Get thee behind me, Satan," Jesus responded when Peter suggested that Jesus not go up to Jerusalem. Peter denied Him three times, running away from his Lord and friend just when Jesus needed him most. A list of Peter's good works looks rather spotty.

Yet here is the man on whom Jesus chose to build His church. Maybe Jesus knew he'd be a good role model for most of us, who also abandon Christ in different ways, who also miss the point, who also lose faith halfway across the lake. The point about Peter's goodness—or lack of it—is most comforting. If God can love and use a man like Peter, there is hope that God loves us and can use us. Jesus didn't die for us because we are good, but because, like Peter, we are sinners.

Peter's story proves that self-earned goodness is not necessary to enter the Kingdom; in fact, the reverse is true—

goodness based on our own estimation keeps the kingdom out. The great, excellent, superb, astonishing news is that God forgives us and restores us to the good, God-given state He created us to live in.

Chapter 8

WORSHIP

Hallelujah! Praise God in his holy temple . . .
Praise him with the blast of the ram's-horn;
praise him with lyre and harp.
Praise him with timbrel and dance;
praise him with strings and pipe.
Praise him with resounding cymbals . . .
Let everything that has breath
praise the Lord. Hallelujah!

—PSALM 150

Toddlers squirmed on the floor, while the older kids and parents sat crowded in folding chairs in the basement community hall after a potluck supper, watching the talent show. Another sixth grader and I had self-consciously sung "Serasponda," and a preadolescent young man with plastered hair and serious, dark-rimmed glasses ground away on his cello.

Suddenly, one of his strings went—boing! And the young man stood up in alarm and dismay, clutching his hand to his chest. He wailed, "I can't go on! My G-string broke!"

My mother and a friend nearly fell off their chairs laughing. Mortified (why would you laugh at the poor guy who was obviously embarrassed beyond words? Besides which, I had a secret crush on him. Also, I had no clue what a G-string was), I glared at my mother in my own preadolescent huff of offense. Now I look back and see the hilarity of the incident—and remember the warmth and fellowship of the evening as well.

This is just one of the many memories I have of family activities at the Quaker church in Richmond, Indiana, where we attended for two years. In contrast to the quiet meeting, Sunday school and family nights were loaded with music and fun. We memorized the books of the Bible, we watched slide shows of real African missionaries in khakis standing by camels and elephants, we met in our teacher's home for a delicious meal and fun and games.

On the quieter side, I also remember another group of Friends, who met on the college campus where my father was a student. Taking a book or a sketch pad was a must for a kid in grade school. How else could you make it through an hour of total silence, broken only occasionally when the Holy Spirit moved this or that adult to speak? Further, the Quakers were so austere in their dress that I didn't have the amusement of judging and cataloging the women's hats I had earlier in the Episcopal church.

I remember silence and light from those meetings—a large, plain room surrounded by plate glass windows and the view of white-columned, red-brick college buildings with stables at the end of the dirt road. To a young girl, the silence felt like being smothered in a room full of cotton. As an adult, I'm sure I would find the silence a blessing.

During our time in Richmond, another friend invited me to attend the Nazarene church during a revival. What a wild and wonderful time! I remember the noise—amens!—bouncing off each other in chorus of refrain while the preacher shouted his melodious, sing-song appeal to give our lives to Jesus. Women swooned at the altar, calling out to Jesus, and the fans—colorful advertisements for a funeral home—were used for all kinds of activities besides fanning, like swatting each other on the sly. I remember escaping from the hot, writhing room and sliding down a large oak banister—and no one caught us. We were free!

We moved from the Quaker community and returned to the Episcopal church where, at age twelve, I was confirmed. I took my vows seriously, pummeling the teacher with impossible biblical questions (if Cain and Abel were the first children, then where did the other people come from in Genesis 4:15 when Cain had to wear his mark "lest any who came upon him should kill him"?) and difficult moral issues (even if I wrote down every bad thing I've done and confessed it, what about the stuff I can't remember? Am I forgiven for that or not?).

I joined the choir and the junior altar guild, and I remember helping to polish brass nameplates and fixtures on the dark wooden pews in the cool nave, speckled with a rainbow of light from stained glass windows. Echoes of Thomas Crammer's images and cadences from The Book of Common Prayer rolled through the congregation and touched my nascent soul while the priest prepared for communion. As an adult, I have stayed at home in the Episcopal church, and we are raising our children in the ritual that still comforts and moves me week in and week out.

I am grateful, though, for my experiences in the other traditions. Silence (Quaker), enthusiasm (Nazarene), and ritual (Episcopal)—three distinct points in a triangle of faith, and the church as a whole is richer because of all these traditions.

Church history has shown me, if nothing else, how blessed we are to live in a country at a time when we have a feast of worship styles to choose from. America offers churches for hand wavers, for quiet observers, for genuflecters; for those who like forty-minute sermons, for those who like ten-minute sermons; for those who like classical music, for those who like guitars, for those who don't like any instruments at all; for those who want an independent church government, for those who belong to a worldwide apostolic system; for those who emphasize Bible study, or prayer, or spirituality, or social justice. Praise God for our diversity!

Unfortunately, problems arise when we stop celebrating other styles of worship, and start worshiping our own. Schisms are the direct result of idolizing something other than God.

Worship

CHURCH HISTORY

The church history classes in seminary held me spellbound. How did we get from a simple carpenter's death and resurrection to the multiple, and sometimes mutually exclusive, systems of worship we have today? How did we move from a unified mind of the church to rigid institutions that arrogantly pronounce: "If you don't do it our way, you won't be saved"? How did the church shatter into the tiny bits of faith scattered over the earth like the aftermath of a collision?

Once in Estes Park, Colorado, we emerged from our car in the church parking lot on a crisp summer morning. Across the street, a man wearing a hand-scrawled sandwich board picketed, ranting about the cruelty of Christians and shaking his puny fist at the God of the universe. He screamed scathing remarks about the Inquisition and the Crusades and the hypocrisy of Christians in general.

How sad, I thought, because in some ways he was right. Seen with a jaundiced eye, church history reads like a tract promoting atheism by contrast, as episode follows episode of stake-burning, beheading, sword-wielding, power-mongering Christians killing or banishing fellow Christians and anyone else they disagreed with.

Unavoidably true; yet the picketing screamer had missed the real point. From the beginning, the church has been made up of human beings who've come together to celebrate God's love and His gift in Christ. As sinners, we

151

continue to wreck God's perfect church; nevertheless, the church is all we have. The church is God's hands and feet in the world, and we are His representatives these days in an increasingly pagan American culture. That is why it is so important that Christians remember to worship God instead of our ideas about how we should worship Him— and to keep our squabbles to a minimum. Like the poor man in Estes Park spouting anti-Christian venom, all you have to do to become cynical is to read the newspapers, smothered with stories of churches and congregations struggling with each other to grab the Truth and lock it up in their own special corner.

At the heart of Christianity is the *kerygma*, the Faith with a capital F summed up in a nutshell: Jesus Christ, Son of God, died for our sins, rose from the dead, and will come again in glory. This testament as revealed in the Bible is what separates Christians from non-Christians. Christians have accepted Jesus Christ as their savior, and non-Christians have not. Baptist, Roman Catholics, Nazarenes, Quakers, Episcopalians, Methodists, Church of Christ congregations, Presbyterians, Lutherans, Disciples of Christ congregations, Bible churches, and all otherwise disconnected worship groups are unified in this Faith.

On a plane once, I sat next to a couple who couldn't have been more different from me—different generation, different race, different clothes, you name it. Yet before the plane took off, we discovered that we shared the most im-

152

portant thing in life. We were all Christians. Though their worship service was completely unlike the Episcopal service, I have no doubt that if that plane had crashed on a desert island, we would have found a way to worship God among the sand and palm trees and been grateful for our small community of believers.

So why are we not one big happy church? Why do we fight even within denominations?

By definition, every Christian accepts the Faith; the Faith is like a soothing refrain, a theme recurring in an otherwise wild and discordant symphony. This essential Faith is not the problem. Two other elements account for the discord, two elements that the church from the beginning has been tempted to worship instead of Jesus: belief (doctrine) and practice (the expression of faith and belief).

After the post-resurrection appearances of Jesus—in the locked room of frightened disciples, at the meal on the beach, and at the festival of Pentecost—the church began to come together in small gatherings loosely based on Jewish synagogue services. Soon questions arose and quarrels broke out, not over the Faith, but over belief and practice. How was Jesus the Son of God? How was God a Trinity? How were we supposed to induct the new members? Who was going to be the boss?

An important thing to remember as we look at the first-century church is that the early church did not get its teaching from the Bible, but vice versa. The New Testament took its form and its substance from the early church members who wrote down the teachings of Jesus, spread orally by the Apostles; but they didn't start writing the stories down until the Apostles started dying off. The early church then decided which of the many written gospels went into the canon, selecting the four we have but deleting others, such as the Gospel of Thomas. Thus, while the church was forming both its liturgy and its structure, it did not have the New Testament to guide it. It had only the discernment of the Holy Spirit and the wisdom of the Apostles.

In fact, if we look closely, the New Testament is the literary documentation of the church's early clashes—monumental quarrels that shaped it. Acts 15 records the first council held to decide the dispute over Gentile circumcision. Whether it's any comfort or not, we see in the Bible that from the beginning, church members have been at each other's throats, struggling to explain and carry out the Faith. And God has always redeemed our efforts, no matter how fractious we become.

BELIEF AND PRACTICE

I'd like to look at the history of one belief and one practice in order to figure out why we fight to the death over non-essentials of the Faith.

Let's take the Lord's Supper, a very different affair from church to church. Some Communions are closed to anyone not a member of a particular denomination, and others are open to everybody. Some Eucharistic theology is a complicated set of beliefs dealing with the elements and their supernatural transformation, and other Eucharistic theology functions as a simple remembrance. And, of course, we see everything in between.

My question here is this: Is any one Eucharistic doctrine exclusively "right"—or worth hurting people over? In Vietnam, the underground church came together for the Lord's Supper at great personal risk. For Communion, they used the only thing they had—a coconut, the meat and the juice representing bread and wine. During World War II in the Pacific, prisoners of war gathered secretly for Communion and used—nothing, except prayer. They had nothing to use because they were being starved to death, so they held out their hands and received air as the Body and Blood of Christ. Were their Communions not valid in God's eyes because they didn't have the proper elements?

Jesus Himself did not spell out theologically what He did at the Last Supper. He said simply, "This is my body. This is my blood." He did not say do this in remembrance once a year, once a month, once a day. He didn't say to use wafers, loaves, or coconuts. He didn't explain what exactly happens to the bread and wine once it is blessed.

No, we are the ones who have tainted a holy thing with our rules of correctness and exclusion.

It could be worse, and was. Originally a full meal was included in the Lord's Supper. The head person blessed, broke, and served the bread—then offered supper to the whole crowd. Imagine a potluck meal in the middle of Communion! Then, after supper, the leader blessed and shared the cup of wine.

The most serious problem was not who was going to bring the fried chicken or the desserts, but the fact that the Gentiles were used to guzzling wine with their meals. As a result, by the second half of the service—to the dismay of the reverent Jewish Christians—Eucharist was a rowdy, drunken party.

Wisely, the church fathers cut out the meal.

We should be so wise. Instead of fighting over wine or grape juice, we should be trying to get the unchurched to the Lord's Table. Any Lord's Table.

Now to examine a doctrine. Has anyone you know ever been involved in a discussion about the literal interpretation of the Bible? Let me rephrase that. Has anyone you know ever been involved in a calm, unemotional, levelheaded discussion over biblical literalism? It's been my experience that unless I'm talking with people who share my views, this issue becomes a hot potato almost before the subject has been introduced.

Nothing changes. The early bishops and scholars at Antioch encouraged a literal and historical reading of the Scriptures. Well and good. However, equally persuasively, the bishops, and scholars at Alexandria promoted an allegorical reading. Early on, the battle lines were drawn, and this issue was not resolved until both cities were overrun by the Mohammedans in the seventh century.

Actually, the battle continues today. In almost two thousand years, neither side has convinced the other. What inevitably takes over is the fiery need to be right, to inform the other side that they are dead wrong and are going to hell for being either too liberal or too narrow-minded.

Taken either literally or metaphorically, the biblical message to love one's neighbor disappears in arguments like this. What I've learned from witnessing and taking part in such discussions is that *it is more important to love your opponent than to win.*

I have noticed a truth of human nature concerning religious beliefs and practices. The more trivial the issue, the greater the heat. Try replacing the blue carpet with red in the sanctuary if you want to see sparks fly.

For me, whenever I feel that surge of anger, or that first level in my wall of defense go up, I try to stop and think. Why am I upset? Am I arguing about the Faith, or do I fear that one of my pet religious idols is being attacked? Usually, whenever my gorge rises in a religious discussion, I find that I am defending something non-essential that I hold too close to my heart.

Love is more important than winning.

HUMAN NATURE

Five aspects of human nature keep us from unity: our lust for power, our resistance to change, our egos, our love of being right, and a temptation toward exclusivity.

Here's a story from my own tradition, a church started by Henry the Eighth. In March 1511, a London tailor-merchant named Richard Hunne lost his infant son. The rector demanded as payment for burial rites the sheet the tiny body was wrapped in. Hunne refused. The rector sued. Hunne countersued on the grounds that the rector had offended the statutes established to protect the English crown against the pope. The upshot was that Hunne was arrested, declared a heretic, and, two days after his imprisonment, found murdered in his cell.

We are a far cry here from the love of Jesus Christ.

Fortunately, we are more tolerant in this century; we no longer murder people routinely for power struggles over faith. But the issue of power is not dead. The contemporary Episcopal church is racked over the issue of the ordination of practicing homosexuals, and I suspect beneath that banner lurks a question of power and a battle over who is going to run our church, the liberals or the conservatives.

See if you recognize any power struggles from the following list:

Deciding on the style of music in the main service

Building a Family Life Center

Firing a secretary

Getting rid of the current youth director

Deciding whether women should participate as leaders in the service.

A priest friend of ours moved from an old church (old by American standards, anyway) where the disputes over the bulletin, the sanctuary lamp, the carpet, and who sat in which pew went back for generations. He moved to a new mission barely begun. *Good,* he thought. *I won't have any of those old codgers digging in their heels over everything, including the way the flag is carried down the aisle.*

He was mistaken. The first time he proposed a slight change in the Christmas Eve service, he discovered that these people were even more violent about change than the old codgers. "You can't change the manger scene! We've done it that way for two years now!"

Flabbergasted (and unwilling to fight over something so trivial), he kept the manger scene "the way they'd always done it."

Human nature balks at change, especially change in an area as meaningful as church ritual. The identification of faith and symbol penetrates deep into our psyches, and we feel spiritually violated when our habits of worship are altered. Still, as we grow in the faith, we come to see that Jesus Christ is the one unchanging element in all we do, and if we keep our eyes fixed on Him, it won't crush us when the vestry votes, for instance, to allow layreaders to wear street clothes instead of robes.

G. K. Chesterton wrote a poem about Palm Sunday. Told from the donkey's point of view, it expresses the donkey's joy when he carried Jesus through the streets. In some senses, a Christian leader is like that donkey carrying a precious passenger on its back. Problems arise when leaders think the cheers are for them instead of for Jesus.

Paul warns the Corinthians against worshiping a particular Christian leader instead of Jesus: "Each one of you says, 'I belong to Paul,' or 'I belong to Apollos,' or 'I belong to Cephas,' or 'I belong to Christ.' Is Christ divided? Was Paul crucified for you?" (1 Cor. 1:12-13). Paul kept his ego reined in, steering his followers toward Christ instead of himself. Likewise so did church leaders such as Jonathan Edwards, George Whitefield, and the Wesleys.

Unfortunately, American church history is also riddled with dynamic leaders, Joseph Smith for example, who collected a small group of followers around them and then split off into a heretical group. Thus separated, with no tradition or hierarchy to keep them in check, leaders assumed Godlike permission to break with important tenets of the true and established Faith. The worst-case scenarios of ego-driven church leaders include David Koresh, Jim Jones, and just recently the leader of Heaven's Gate, all of whom eventually led many of their smitten followers to their deaths.

The church splinters when we follow anyone else but Jesus.

❧

Is anything more immediately delicious than being right? After all, who likes eating humble pie? In religious matters, it's not just being right we love, but we love being right because we confuse being right with being righteous. Of course, we cannot see ourselves slipping from the grace-filled pool of righteousness into the somewhat slimier pond of self-righteousness; we cannot see the sludge of pride adhering to our opinions—though others have a great view of the muck invisible to us.

We train our young ones in our particular tradition, and we should. What we shouldn't do is give our children subliminal messages along with the Bible stories we teach: This is the right way to do things. Real Christians kneel. Or real Christians don't read prayers from a book. Or real Christians baptize by immersion. Or real Christians have to profess publicly. People who don't do it our way aren't real Christians.

We are right and they are wrong.

Being right is not like a two-sided coin, with wrong on the opposite side. Being right can also be like a sphere with two round hemispheres; as you travel around to the other side of the globe, you discover that it isn't wrong over there, but it is also right—from a different perspective.

The Inquisition started out being right. By 1572, Protestantism was extinct in Italy. The Puritans started out being right, too. We all remember the witch-hunts that resulted.

Being right can be a deadly proposition.

In fact, we need to fear being right more than being tolerant. Seeking right, seeking pat answers, seeking to peg God leads inevitably to fear and closed-mindedness. The ability to accept God's mystery and the ability to relinquish the need to be right are two helpful skills in working toward peace in the Kingdom of Heaven on earth. The minute we're convinced we're right, we're into idolatry.

Again, it is more important to love your opponent than to win an argument.

One caveat, however. Tolerance, like every other God-given quality, works best in moderation. Discernment is necessary so that tolerance does not mean "anything goes." Too much tolerance, like too much narrow-mindedness, can become an idol also, and steer the church away from Christ.

⌒

The final characteristic that causes us to worship our own form of worship is the desire for exclusivity. C. S. Lewis calls it the "phenomenon of the Inner Ring."[1] It is this phenomenon which creates private schools, country clubs, and circles within circles.

The Gnostics were the first Christian "in crowd." They separated themselves from the masses who accepted simple Christianity, claiming that they had secret, more elaborate information about the faith, known only to those who joined their elite group.

They were also the first heretics.

Current temptations for exclusivity sometimes include those who have accepted Jesus under certain conditions, who speak a special religious jargon, who've been to certain colleges and schools, or who've been to renewal weekends like Cursillo or the Walk to Emmaus. Renewal groups are wonderful, Spirit-filled experiences which bring many languishing Christians back to life. However, sometimes an attitude of exclusivity sneaks in: Those who've been on such a weekend (or to such a school, or who talk a certain way) now possess a more "authentic" faith.

Thus we begin to worship our own experience.

Jesus came to save us all. In the Kingdom of Heaven, bishops and new converts are on equal footing, as are the wealthy and the poor, the handwavers and the pew sitters, Cursillistas on fire and crustaceans baptized eighty years ago.

This Easter a local news station broadcast a story with clips from both an Hispanic Roman Catholic congregation and a Bible church congregation. I got goose bumps at the result. The story was a foretaste of the Kingdom, filled with praise and not bickering. The two services couldn't have contrasted more greatly in style, but the message on both sides came out loud and clear: Jesus is risen! Praise God!

IN CONCLUSION

The church of Christ is a large and mighty fleet of ships, much like the fleet of diverse boats that set out from Dover to rescue the men from Dunkirk in World War II. England rounded up any craft that floated to send across the channel. Besides destroyers and cruisers from the Royal Navy, the British conscripted all kinds of other ships, such as fishing smacks, drifters, excursion boats, motor launches, tugs towing lifeboats, Thames sailing barges, cabin cruisers, dredges, trawlers, and rust-streaked scows.

This motley fleet set out under intense enemy fire with one united goal: to save the lives of thousands of British and French soldiers.[2]

Like this unlikely rescue operation, the church of God steams across time, under fire from a far more subversive and dangerous enemy. This enemy delights in the potshots we take at each other because our in-fighting detracts from our true common goal, that of leading to Christ souls drowning in apathy, discord, despair, and unbelief. We simply cannot afford to lose sight of the Captain of the fleet.

Chapter 9

EASE

Come to me, all who labor and are heavy laden, and I will give you rest.
—MATTHEW II:28

The phone call came when Anita had just doused the toilet in the twins' bathroom with disinfectant. Cradling the receiver against her shoulder, she swished inside the bowl with her trusty brush, then sprayed another coat of disinfectant on the seat.

Four thousand dollars they owed the government. Four thousand dollars Anita had squirreled away to pay the staggering bill at the twins' special school for kids with severe dyslexia.

Anita told the accountant "Thank you" in the most sincere voice she could muster, flicked off the phone, and sank onto the tile floor, leaning her back against the tub. Unable to resist the itch any longer, she scratched her hives (an eternal curse, she feared, going on six weeks) under her jeans, knowing full well the hot fire that would spread up her thighs and down to her ankles.

It was Holy Week. Her husband, an ordained minister, would be swamped at church, with a broken copier and an unexpected funeral service, frantic for time to write his Good Friday and Easter sermons. She should wait to tell him until after Easter, but what, oh, what were they going to do?

Leaving the toilet brush dangling like a spoon in a soup bowl, Anita buried her head and wept, streaks of pain shooting up and down the skin on her legs.

How about a break, Lord? Just one little tiny break?

She should trust God more, be less prone to depression, she chided herself, smearing mascara all over her cheeks. Or maybe the problem lay in her childhood, having been raised with certain expectations. Her own mother had never cleaned a toilet in her life. But her mother hadn't married a clergyman, either.

The twins. What were they going to do? They had failed in the public schools, and Anita had home-schooled them one semester (a disaster—she was a lousy teacher). She had located a school in the next county where they were finally, at age nine, learning to read. But the cost was killing her.

Anita wanted desperately to get a job, but her husband

had been called to a church in a town too small to provide work for one more real estate agent. At her wits' end, she had applied to work at the local Wal-Mart; but her husband had fallen gravely ill, and she had to nurse him for several months after his emergency surgery.

Reluctantly, Anita picked up the toilet brush and gave it one last listless swish. Last summer, determined not to let her circumstances defeat her, she had started her own computer business, creating web sites for several clients she had worked hard to cultivate all over the state.

That was the problem. She had pinched pennies and scraped together four thousand dollars from her business after paying off her husband's hospital bills, and now the government wanted it all; because she was self-employed, the government added on an extra tax, a fact she hadn't fully realized though she had suspected she would owe the IRS a little something in April.

Anita flushed the toilet and watched the blue liquid swirl out of sight. Gone, she thought, just like the money.

In the kitchen, she scarfed down five chocolates from the sampler she'd bought on sale after Valentine's Day. God would handle this, she knew.

But why, oh, why was her life so unrelentingly difficult?

Just as the last chocolate dissolved into a soothing pool in her mouth, she sniffed an odor like burning plastic coming from the air vent, right before the heater went rattle, rattle, chug, boom, and died.

THE PROMISES OF CHRIST

My husband's grandmother used to say cheerfully, "If it's not one thing . . . it's two." A graciously aging matriarch, Momo had accepted the fact that life was bumpy and that nothing worked quite as well or smoothly as the guarantee claimed. In fact, I remember Momo as a woman of good humor, smiling serenely while macular degeneration took her eyesight. Although aware of the price of Easter, she always managed to focus on the Resurrection, even when the events in her own life went sour. Her trust in God was almost childlike (a goal for us all) in its fullness and depth.

Momo's faith operated like a set of shock absorbers in tip-top condition. In contrast, many people I know (including myself) tend to feel every pothole, every rock in the road. Traveling down the road of life, we are bounced, thrown against the dashboard, run off the road, wrecked by oncoming trains; we run out of gas, suffer flat tires, and collide with drunk drivers.

In short, life is not easy.

Why not?

As I have tackled each chapter in this book, I have thought, in succession, *This chapter is the one that deals with my worst problem.* However, as I began this chapter on the idol of ease, I thought, *This chapter really deals with my worst problem.* The difficulty, I think, lies in the premise. Instead of assuming life should be easy and wondering why it's not, we should be asking the question, "Why on earth do we expect life to be easy in the first place?"

Through the culture, Satan seduces us into thinking that life should be easy. Because for many of us life is *not* easy, we have trouble reconciling its difficulty and pain with our expectation of comfort and convenience. We must be doing something wrong. We must not be "good" enough Christians. But why do we expect ease as our due? The Bible is filled with people who struggled, and many who died for their faith. Jesus Himself said that our lives as Christians would be difficult. God fills our lives with challenges, not bonbons, because it is the challenges that bring us closer to Him and ultimately bring us joy.

Last week for me was a week similar to Anita's, and my response to our particular set of disasters brought into the light how much I would like life to be easy. I fantasize about a Christian plateau, just above the plane of my actual spiritual life, where dryers never break, where clergy husbands aren't run ragged, where little children are not forced to learn so young the rules of the jungle, and where I am perfectly content with whatever God has put on my plate.

Last week, I realized (again) that the problem was not the small avalanche of troubles that had recently rolled downhill and left rocks strewn. No, there will always be rocks and potholes in the road. The problem was my attitude. Instead of spending so much time complaining and trying by myself to dislodge boulders, I should be inside the car praying, asking God to help me navigate through the rubble.

My focus was on the irritating external events, not on my inner response. God will handle it. I must learn to let Him.

The problem is that we don't take Jesus seriously on two counts. First, we don't really believe Him when He says, "You'll have trouble in the world" (John 16:33). Never does He say, "If you believe in Me, life will be a piece of cake." Instead He promises *tribulation*—as defined in the Random House Dictionary, "grievous trouble; severe trial or suffering." Not fun and games, not pure joy, not an easy life.

Second, we don't take Him seriously when He says to be of good cheer *in spite of the pain.* He has overcome any glitches, sadness, and exhaustion life hands us, from broken appliances to death. He really means this, but we don't believe Him; instead, we throw ourselves elaborate and expensive pity parties about the difficulty of life.

The challenge that this week brought me was how to claim the second promise of Christ, how to let Him change my attitude so that I'm not thrown out of the car when it crashes into life's debris on the road.

THE NO-WARRANTY CLAUSE

Most pieces of new equipment—dishwashers, air conditioners, egg beaters, cars—come with a warranty. The manufacturer promises that the item will work properly for up to a year (or more). If a part fails, or something goes wrong with the equipment, the manufacturer guarantees to replace or fix the item free of charge, as long as the owner fills in the little 3x5 card and sends it in upon purchase.

You see, the manufacturers want to keep the customer happy, not for the sake of our happiness, but so we will continue to buy their products. When our hair dryer blows up (approximately one week after the warranty expires, of course), the manufacturers want us to buy another hair dryer from them. The guarantee policy actually has the manufacturer's best interest at heart, though it may seem to keep the customer's best interest up front.

As adults, we enter life with the warranty mentality. Somewhere in the back of our minds we believe that our lives should work properly, should function the way we want them to. When things go wrong, we feel somebody owes us a new part, a fresh start, a different set of circumstances. Life is harder than we reckon, and we wonder, Where is the guarantee? What happened to the clause that says, "I will fix the problem free of charge"?

God, our manufacturer, has a different agenda from the agenda of the makers of, say, potato peelers. Whereas manufacturers ultimately keep their own interests and the bottom line in mind, God has our genuine, deepest best interests in mind. He knows a little secret about human nature since the Fall. When things are too easy for too long, we tend to mildew spiritually and fall away from Him.

Instead of entering life with the warranty mentality, we should read the fine print and start our journeys understanding a different kind of promise. It goes something like this: Yes, your oven will go out, most likely right before thirty relatives and friends arrive for Thanksgiving dinner. Your children will not understand you and vice versa. Your car will break down the morning of your most important business meeting. Most of you will never have enough money, and those who do may well be haunted by a sense of guilt and ennui. Your husband will always leave the toilet seat up. Your wife will complain about the same old things year after year. Your migraines will return, you will develop diabetes, your children will require trips to the emergency room. Further, many of these things will happen all at once.

This is the first part of life's agreement, the fine print we all ignore in our eagerness to be adults: In the world, you have tribulation.

The second part of the Christian's life agreement is the good news and what we need to focus on. When we give ourselves to Christ, He redeems all the crummy stuff life tries to defeat us with. Jesus supersedes Murphy's law and all its miserable corollaries.

The spiritual challenge is to live as though this were true, instead of just a Sunday saying framed on our wall, displayed but not lived out. Jesus made these promises so that we are not stuck in despair, surrounded by the broken

machinery of life. Though it is our fingers which do the
dialing and we who have to deal with the frustrations of
expensive electricians, plumbers who run four hours late,
or whatever else has gone wrong, Jesus helps us from the
inside. He gives us patience, He soothes our irritated spirits, He even leads us to ways we can, after all, afford the
repairs. We take our inner brokenness to Him so He can
fix it, and we can live in His peace. He doesn't promise no
problems, no pain. He promises to help us repair the internal damage to our spirits, and He also leads us and guides
us through the worldly machinations of life's problems.
Just when we think we can't afford to repair the dishwasher,
He sends a little surprise. Maybe it's money from an unexpected source—a gift, or a refund, or a friend who offers to
fix it for free. Or maybe He gives us extra time to pray as
we wash the dishes by hand.

I picture Jesus in a worker's apron standing behind a
counter in a shop cluttered with bits and pieces of all of
life's junk. A sign above the fix-it shop's door says, "Wel-
come. Open twenty-four hours a day. Will give you patience
and inspiration to help heal everything from broken washing machines to broken hearts. May take longer than
expected. Situation may not look as you originally planned.
But redemption of some sort guaranteed."

If we turn over the problem to Jesus, we don't have to
tinker uselessly with it, growing more and more desperate
and irritated. After we make the necessary phone calls, we

can rest, knowing that somehow, some way, He will help us fix the situation. True, He may not resolve the problem on our terms; but as the sign says, He guarantees redemption in some form. Jesus has overcome the world.

A few summers ago, my children and I developed an intestinal parasite from bottled water, of all things. My husband, who drank the city's tap water (containing more chlorine than a swimming pool) did not get this giardia. In order to confirm my son's case, I had to take a specimen to the doctor's. As I carried his little potty down the stairs, I tripped and pulled a muscle in my neck. Oh, well, I thought. It could have been worse. I could have spilled the potty contents all over myself and the rug.

That weekend, the washing machine went out. Anyone with a four-year-old and a baby both with intestinal parasites knows that a washing machine is essential to life. We couldn't wait to buy a new one, but we couldn't afford one either. So my husband trekked out in the rain while I nursed my neck (and my own giardia) and made little piles of soiled laundry. He found an industrial size machine on sale, which he had to bring home in the back of the minivan because the company didn't deliver sale items. The only problem was that the van died by the side of the road, with the washer strapped on the back. In the rain.

Several weeks later, after three of us had caught—and shared—the stomach virus (on top of the lingering giardia), my grandmother died.

When the car went out *again,* I said, Lord? hello? hello? is anybody there?

This past week, we had a fresh slew of problems, including my pinkie finger, which was sliced to the bone; a twenty-five-year-old air conditioning system that we can now use for a heater; an unpleasant surprise, like Anita's, from the IRS; and, among other pressing parish problems, yet another death, which means sadness for many and, for the consolation committee, putting on our fifteenth funeral reception in as many weeks.

Physical pain, emotional pain, financial pain. I seem bankrupt in all three areas. I am sad about the death, irritated because my finger hurts as I prepare food for the funeral reception; and like many Americans, we will be borrowing money to avoid jail on the one hand, and a scalding Texas summer on the other.

One of these days, when I am spiritually mature, I will be able to shrug my shoulders with instant peace, smile serenely, and say, "Jesus is handling all these things. I'm not concerned at all." In the meantime, I am about halfway there. Still typing in pain from the sliced finger, I have to admit to a certain amount of irritation, sadness, depression; I am still bristling at having to face so many things at once. It seems as though the grim reaper is visiting our parish far too regularly, bringing down general morale. I chafe at having to borrow money for the air conditioner at a ridiculous interest rate. Instead of allowing the correct spiritual response to wing its way into my soul instantly and automatically, I have to remind my sluggish spirit of Matthew 11:28: "Oh, yes. Jesus promised to give me rest from these burdens. He will take care of all these things if I give them to Him."

With surprise and gratitude, I also have to admit to moments when I am at peace. Jesus is here, in the middle of the mess, and sometimes I can almost feel His presence palpably, laughing at my silly humanness. He saw us through the summer of giardia. He will see us through this.

Jesus will not fix our air conditioning, I know that. Jesus will not make four dozen deviled eggs for me. Jesus will not float dollar bills like manna on our front lawn. I have spent many hours on the phone with credit managers and have more hours ahead dealing with service people. I may even be facing the necessity of getting another part-time job to pay off the loan.

I wish this person hadn't died. I wish that the air conditioner had never broken, or that God had miraculously fixed it. I also wish that Jesus promised to make us feel good once we ask Him for help. But that's not the promise. The promise is that Jesus will be there with us in the middle of the problem. God doesn't take away the chafing of the world; rather, His refreshment is the lotion after a scrub down with sandpaper on the skin.

In Joanna Trollope's novel *The Rector's Wife*, the archdeacon tells Anna, who has come to him with a life filled with lumps and pain, "The noblest bravery is battling against these dreadful daily assaults, often very minor, on one's spirit."[1] Life won't be easy. Life won't feel good. But eventually, all will be absorbed into the promise of Christ's presence. The noblest bravery is endurance.

There. Even as I type, I have noticed a slight improvement in my finger.

THE IDEAL LIFE

"To be alive is to have problems."[2] So where did we get the idea in the first place that life should be trouble free? Is this an age-old human illusion or a more recent twentieth-century ideal?

Journals, autobiographies, and diaries from the past several centuries detail the harshness of life for many people, especially the lower classes. Disease often wiped out one's whole brood of children. Crops failed. The milk cow died, and the plow horse broke his leg. Slum landlords kicked families out onto the streets to beg. Even among upper classes, the harshness of life killed off most of the population before what we consider middle age.

In *On the Banks of Plum Creek,* part of her famous *Little House on the Prairie* series, Laura Ingalls Wilder tells of a locust storm that wiped out the family's entire wheat crop one afternoon. In vivid detail, she tells of a "glittering cloud" that swarmed through the farm, eating everything inside and outside the house, leaving stains even on the girls' Sunday dresses. As the family watched their lives and livelihood destroyed in one fell swoop, they also observed the chickens, gorging on the locusts. "'Well, we won't have to buy feed for the hens,' said Ma. 'There's no great loss without some gain.'"[3]

Writers didn't tell stories like this so that we would feel sorry for the harshness of life for people back then. Self-pity is not an undercurrent. For these writers, simple observation proved that life was short and severe, but they wanted to underscore the message that they could and did overcome difficulties.

Only recently, it seems, do we feel life owes us.

The more power we have gained over death, over circumstance, over physical labor, the more we feel we deserve only the best. Our culture has cloaked the undeniable—unavoidable—truth that life is hard, disguising its burdens with glittering expectations we have concocted from advertising, bad logic, and sheer desire.

We are born into antiseptic rooms attended by specialists, and we are instantly incubated at the first sign of trouble. We are no longer pushed into the soft down of our mother's bed at home, with an aunt or a midwife washing and swaddling us lovingly, gingerly. The trade-off is better health: We are also not surrounded by germs and ignorance. Today, most babies (and mothers) survive the dangerous tunnel of birth. But because the percentage of survival is so high, we lull ourselves into thinking a safe and easy birth is our due. We now consider death from childbirth a cruel aberration, instead of the normal risk it once was.

Ditto for childhood diseases. I'm old enough to remember the danger of polio. Polio permanently weakened my oldest cousin and crippled or killed others. Mothers now take for granted that childhood diseases are mostly inconveniences, not the killers they once were. Life owes us. We are so clever, we can beat off death.

A quick look in the archives of national magazines like *Life* reveals the progression of ease in the area of household and office chores. Again, within my lifetime, calculators have replaced slide rules and troublesome sums done in one's own brain. I wrote my master's thesis on an old-fashioned typewriter, and now I often wonder how I suffered through the experience. My mother had to wash the dishes with no dishwasher, and my grandfather had to pump by foot his dentist's drill. You get the point. Each decade life gets easier mechanically, until we think we are being punished when the dishwasher breaks, or the computer dies.

At the same time, forces beyond our control are also at work in the other direction. The AIDS virus remains unharnassed, even by our smartest scientists. No matter how sophisticated the computers in our cars become, we cannot eradicate car trouble. No pension or insurance plan can cover all emergencies.

We are outraged when our life experience is difficult. Machines should work (but they don't). Everyone should live their three-score and ten years (but they don't). Accidents should be preventable (but they aren't). We are "shoulding" ourselves to death! Where is it coming from, this discrepancy between reality and our expectations?

According to the *New York Times*, the average American encounters approximately three thousand ads a day—all giving us the unvarying message that we are special, but with a twist. Jeanie Wylie-Kellerman elaborates: "You are special *but* you are not getting what you deserve. 'It's a shame,' the advertisers tell you, 'that you don't have what makes these people so happy. You deserve it. And with credit, you can have it now.'"[4]

We are fed a steady diet not only of the message that instant gratification is best (another idol altogether), but that the wonderful, easy, pain-free life we deserve is within our reach. This theme appeals to us on several levels. It's not just the easy life we seek, but we also want to believe the subliminal message that we can control our lives. All we need is money.

Our culture has been called in certain intellectual circles "post-Christian." I seriously doubt the truth of this statement. However, our culture is certainly not pervasively Christian, and it is important for Christians to be aware of the deep non-Christian undercurrents we are fighting. Until we can recognize and separate the influences working on us, our spirituality will suffer, and we won't really know why.

Ads are so dangerous because they start with a basic human truth. Yes, we are special. We are special because God made us. However, the snake convinces us that we do not deserve an easy life simply because we were created. When we cannot accept the difficulty of life, when we pray only for God to remove pain and obstacles, we miss the point. We worship a God who comes to us in our pain. Our God overcomes tribulation; He doesn't remove it. He also helps us discern where the enemy leads us astray in our thinking so that we don't worship the carefree lives we see in the ads.

For instance, I am a sucker for old movies on TV, which means I endure a lot of car ads. Cars are not my thing. I want a vehicle that works; I don't care what it looks like. So the ads where the road talks, where the pigeon crashes into the garage door squawking "Mayday," and where the effete guy tries to smooth talk me into a luxury car—those ads simply roll off my back. Also, I tune out the ads for clothes, jewelry, trucks, boots, and cotton fertilizer.

The cruise ads are a different story. Watching the couple dancing in the moonlight, bathing by the pool, eating that midnight buffet makes me long, yearn for just one week in the Caribbean. The raw power of ads is frightening. I have often wondered what a simple hamburger ad looks like to a starving person. Ads tell us things we do not need to hear.

Another cultural reason our generation chafes so at the

difficulty of life is that our parents, children of the depression, sought to pave the way for us—materially, educationally, and socially—with every advantage. They didn't want us to have to suffer as they did growing up. As a result, we are flat spoiled. We look to life to give us all the toys and popsicles we want, because our parents did.

Our personal lives appear difficult because we are tempted to compare our lot with the lot of those around us—always a dangerous and empty business. With a few notable exceptions, most people seem to live easier lives than we do. There goes Susie Smith. She inherited half a million dollars, and she never has financial worries. Her husband dotes on her. She's never been sick a day in her life. Lucky Susie Smith. Of course, we don't know about Susie's battle with alcoholism, or the fact that the wealthy father who left her money also left her scars from burning her small feet with cigarette butts.

Again, the archdeacon in *The Rector's Wife* offers a snippet of wisdom. He comments, it is "so odd that humanity declines, on the whole, to think that other people are as human as itself."[5] We are all in it together. If we think someone else has a clearer path, a smoother road, well, maybe they do. But more likely, they do not. As my colleague and friend Dr. Pamela Howell says, if we are going to envy someone, we need to envy the whole package, not just one particularly attractive aspect of someone's life. For all we know, someone may be envying something about us.

I used to know a woman who related story after miracle story from what appeared to be the jewel-studded crown of her spiritual life. A group of us used to sit around, discussing the hardships of our respective ministries, asking for prayer to survive discouragement and doors closed in our faces. This woman countered with victory after victory in her ministry, saying breezily, "God was looking out after me." A friend commented wryly, "I wonder what it would be like to have all your prayers expedited like that. God seems to go ahead of her like a nineteenth-century Victorian street sweeper; you know, those little boys who'd scurry in front of ladies in long dresses, clearing a path across the dirt roads."

I had to remind myself that this woman had faced hardship in other ways, at other times. Envy was a temptation for the rest of us, in the face of our own particular and immediate difficulties. Only with God's grace were we able to praise God for her life and what He was doing through her.

The false, but seemingly inevitable, conclusion in comparison is that God loves some more than others, which is not true. That is why comparing is so dangerous.

The ease of life is not a measure of how much God does or doesn't love us. He shows us His love in different arenas of our lives. Comparison is destructive because we either conclude we're better, based on how easy life is on our stretch of the road, or think God loves us less because we face obstacles and are stuck with a derelict vehicle. God loves us all, more than we can know.

Henry Adams is a key figure in American literature, his life span connecting this century with the last. Grandson of John Quincy Adams and great-grandson of John Adams, he lived a privileged but anguished life of transition between the old world and the new. During his lifetime, the United States shifted in several important ways—from an agricultural to an urban society, for example. Henry Adams wrote an autobiography in which he discussed the dynamo, on exhibit in the Paris Exhibition of 1900, as the symbol of the new moral force demanding our obedience. The end result, he predicted, was a headlong rush into chaos and uncontrolled technological power.

The symbol of the dynamo replaced the medieval power of St. Mary, or the earlier Christian power of the cross. St. Mary and the cross provided earlier societies with a moral force energizing their lives. In contrast, the dynamo (and the new technology it represents) offers us the possibility of utopia on earth. The dangers inherent in the expectation of an earthly utopia create spiritual problems like the worship of ease. "Why not?" we ask. If it's within our grasp, we deserve it. "Jim Bob has an easy life. Why not me?"

This is not the Christian message. The Bible tells us in Job, "Man that is born of a woman is of few days, and full of trouble. He comes forth like a flower, and withers; he flees like a shadow, and continues not" (14:1)—a message hard for modern ears. Yet that sums up a great deal . . . except for the cross. Though our human situation is much like Job describes—short but not always sweet—because of Christ, we do experience sprinkles of joy, islands of peace. Jesus promises to be with us in trouble and to help us overcome difficulty. To use another World War II analogy, He does not promise us easy lives of surf, sun, and tropical drinks on a Pacific island, but rather He hunkers down with us in the bunkers of His love, even as bombs from the enemy fall all around us.

Chapter 10

UNDERSTANDING

*Now faith is the assurance (the confirma-
tion, the title deed) of the things [we] hope
for, being the proof of things [we] do not
see, and the conviction of their reality—
faith perceiving as real fact what is not
revealed to the senses.*

—HEBREWS 11:1, AB

At the end of the Renaissance pro-
duction of the play *Dr. Faustus,*
grotesque red devils carry the brilliant
Wittenberg scholar off the stage, sting-
ing and torturing him like snakes and
adders. The Mouth of Hell rages with
realistic fingers of flames and blasts from
recently invented gunpowder. The audience, paralyzed with fear, waits for the
moral to be delivered in the final scene,
spelled out in case the playgoers are too
terrified to glean the message from the
hellfire and damnation exploding around

187

them. When the smoke clears, Faustus's fellow scholars emerge and warn the audience: Wise people do not hanker after God's knowledge and understanding. Wise people are content merely to wonder in awe of heavenly ways. The horrific fate of Dr. Faustus awaits those who yearn to know too much.

Ironically, some of his contemporaries accused the playwright, Christopher Marlowe, of atheism; however, his play conveys in graphic terms the Christian message that people who try to play God suffer dearly. Marlowe cautions his fellow Renaissance humanists that their pride of knowledge and understanding has consequences for the soul. Throughout the play, a good angel and a fallen angel battle for the soul of Faustus, who stands for the epitome of the Renaissance scholar—and who finally, in defiance of God, stabs himself in the arm and, with his own blood, signs a pact with Lucifer.

Faustus obsesses over possessing the power of God, over seeing the earth and the universe from God's point of view. At one level, he wants magical powers to make spirits fetch splendid and valuable things for him, priceless goods like pearls and gold and (interestingly) fresh fruit, normally unattainable for him. But he also has a deeper and more complicated desire: He wants all ambiguities explained.[1]

The central theme of *Dr. Faustus* reminds me of Genesis 3. Two other people were also tempted to possess Godlike knowledge and understanding, represented by a piece of fruit glinting in the sunlight on a forbidden tree. In both cases, the participants got what they wanted. In Act III, Mephistopheles whisked Faustus away on a supernatural tour of the cosmos, revealing all the secrets of the universe to him. Adam and Eve also got at least a partial understanding of good and evil. However, the price in both cases—eternal damnation for one, banishment and death for the others—proved to be far greater than either party bargained for.

So what does Dr. Faustus's story have to do with us? In the twentieth century, with one click of the mouse printers regurgitate much of the scientific, cosmological information for which Faustus sold his soul. Fresh fruit is flown in daily to supermarkets; bargain stores feature displays of pearls and gold at prices available to anyone with credit.

In spite of our current smorgasbord of knowledge, still we desire more. Though science and technology enable us to chart and predict natural disasters such as hurricanes, tornadoes, and earthquakes, we still cannot control them. Though we have explained the psychological and sociological causes and effects of good and evil, we cannot keep evil from infiltrating our lives. We cannot grasp the why that haunts us when senseless tragedy razes our carefully constructed houses of comprehension. Like Dr. Faustus, we demand to understand that which is out of our reach.

Seeking understanding is one thing—demanding it is another. Knowledge and understanding become idols when our craving for answers comes before our love of God. The serpent lures us, like Eve, to know more than we can handle. One of the prayers at the end of the Communion service asks that we may grow in the knowledge and love of God, but this is a different prayer from insisting that we understand everything that happens to us. As we grow in knowledge and love of God, we also grow to understand His ways. But to require answers without knowing and loving God is to get things backward.

Even though we know better, we still lust for answers. We are tempted to worship understanding on three levels. First, personal events in our own lives baffle us and threaten to destroy our faith if we can't wrap our hands around a reason for them. Second, the world presents disasters with which we seek to come to terms. We let our horror at the evil displayed around the globe prevent us from accepting a God who claims to be loving and omnipotent but still allows these things to happen. Third, the cosmos itself defies our understanding and gives us no final proof of the kind that science demands. At the root of why we question the ways of God is our struggle to understand evil. At all three levels, we must, finally, take a leap of faith in the face of many unanswered questions.

PERSONAL UNDERSTANDING

Lena, old and crumpled, held the crinkled tissue to her nose like a faded white carnation. "It's not Bobby's fault he's in jail again. He got in with a bad lot last time." Bobby had called his grandmother at 2:30 in the morning to try to con her into bailing him out. Lena, bony and defeated, now sat in the corner of her pastor's couch. "I don't have any money left. Bobby's bail last time used up my retirement. Of course, it wasn't his fault he skipped town. The child's never had a fair deal since his mama ran off with that choir director when Bobby was just a little bitty thing."

The pastor sighed. He remembered Bobby as a kindergartner with a blond crew cut and high-water jeans, stealing matches from the children's chapel and setting fire to the rack of red choir robes. Even then his grandmother denied it. "Bobby couldn't possibly have done that," she cried, ignoring his singed tennis shoes.

Father Smith said, "Lena, jail might be the best thing for Bobby right now. Maybe it's time he took responsibility for his actions. Bail this time—if the judge grants bail at all—will be monstrously expensive. Tying up the clerk and shooting her in the knees, for sixty-seven dollars cash, isn't just stealing. Not this time." Goose bumps silently traveled up and down Father Smith's arms. "It's time we faced the fact that there's something wrong with Bobby."

"Why?" howled Lena suddenly, her face carved with deep lines from years of pain. "Bobby's all I have. I did my best. Why?"

The pastor sighed again and patted her veiny hand. What should he say? He could point out that Lena had raised the child since age five to believe he could do no wrong. The child-rearing books all said that denying children responsibility for their actions is the fastest way to send them to jail. Or he could offer to pray for Bobby's soul. Actually, he'd been praying for Bobby since the incendiary incident in the choir room. Or he could say simply that God's ways were inscrutable.

"I don't know, Lena, sometimes we have to accept on faith that—"

"Not good enough this time." Lena stuffed the used tissue up her sleeve and gathered her purse primly. She struggled up off the couch and smoothed her floral dust coat. "I need answers. I'm eighty-three, and I've devoted my life first to Bobby's mama, then to Bobby. Why me? I can't let the government take him from me. I'll die a lonely, old woman." Lena hobbled out of the pastor's office with her walker.

When Father Smith went to her house the next day, he discovered she had fallen and broken her hip during the night. He visited her regularly at the hospital during the next month, watching her body shrivel and her spirit become warped and bitter. Her thin lips disappeared as she hissed in a whisper, "God has deserted me. It's all been a hoax. I don't believe He loves me anymore." Bobby called her only once, to ask for cigarettes. He hung up when she said she couldn't get to the store.

After Lena died, Father Smith touched the gnarled hand

and prayed that all the answers to Lena's questions would be revealed in the splendor of Christ.

As a clergyman, my husband gets the question "Why me?" flung at him by people in all kinds of circumstances. Cancer. Blindness. Loss of spouse. Loss of job. Loss of limb. For most of us, the demand to know why is a necessary stage in dealing with grief. The anguished cry, "Why, why, why?" belted out to God expresses our anger and pain at the unacceptable. As we work through grief, we need to express our agony to the Lord. If we are open to God's presence and persistent in prayer, we eventually resolve the despair in some manner we can live with—whether or not we get a satisfactory answer to "Why?"

I have witnessed people who, like Lena, become so bitter against God that they do die, shrouded by their unwillingness to accept what may be unanswerable. Though asking "Why?" is a normal and necessary part of recovering from a tragedy, the temptation is to stay there until we are satisfied with the answers. Past a certain point in the grieving process, every time we demand "Why?" we place another brick between ourselves and the Almighty, walling ourselves into a lonely place of self-induced spiritual starvation.

I can remember being tempted not to rest until I understood why. When I was twenty-four, my father left my mother, bursting our image as a happy Christian family. Though I was technically an adult, I remember lying in bed in my lonely apartment feeling like a grenade had hit the campfire my family huddled around for security. Our family now consisted of dismembered body parts flung in all directions. I thought the pain would last the rest of my life. Mother had boxed up our vacation beach home, and I had visions of spending the rest of our holidays bravely trying not to cry, sitting around a bedraggled Christmas tree in a strange house.

As I lay alone in my apartment, the need to know why bored through my being like a drill. I spent several years after the debacle searching for acceptable reasons. Why does any marriage break up? Psychological instability? Selfishness? Boredom? Infidelity? Grandiosity? The hypothetical possibilities were like huge puzzle pieces, none of which fit together to make a coherent picture.

At some point, I decided to get on with my life. I slowly began to drive away from the problem. As is true many times, getting some distance and perspective on the situation helped. Now that twenty-one years have passed, though I still don't understand, I see how God has redeemed a great deal that I thought unredeemable at the time.

Human craving for understanding is associated, as in Faustus's case, with power—or rather the loss of it. Lena had tried to raise Bobby "right." She had taken him to church, loved him in the only way she knew how. Yet she found herself powerless over his grown-up behavior. As a child of divorcing parents, I was a victim of circumstances out of my control. Cancer victims do not plan for their disease; accidents catch us off guard; and death, even expected death, takes survivors' breath away with its finality.

And so we fling our outraged "whys?" heavenward, suffering not only the pain of the loss itself but the more unspeakable pang piercing the illusion that we are masters of our destinies. "You owe me an explanation!" we shout to the Lord of the universe in our powerless rage. If we cannot have things the way we want, then—though it is a poor second choice—we demand to know why things went awry. Starved for answers, we read books like *When Bad Things Happen to Good People.* We need to know, we have a right to know, why life is unfair. We base our demands on the assumptions that we are good, that the thing that has happened to us is bad, and that life should be fair—none of which is necessarily true. But we are too outraged to see.

Squaring off with God occurs in two stages. First, we ask for what we think we need: answers. Then (whether we receive them or not), if these answers allow God to help us probe ourselves and the terrible thing more deeply, He gives us what we're really asking for: meaning.

We think we want a certified, rational, cause-and-effect accounting. We honestly believe a thorough explanation of the reasons behind the painful event will restore some of our lost power. If we participate through comprehension, then we give a permission of sorts for the event to have occurred. Understanding, we think, allows us God's own perspective on things—because from our perspective the thing should never have happened in the first place.

Another reason we desire a cause-and-effect accounting is that we cannot stand the thought of random violence and destruction. A bus wreck kills twenty rosy-cheeked kindergartners. Cells blossom suddenly, darkly out of control. A robbery goes wrong, with blood-spattered walls. If we can ferret out a cause, then we can continue the illusion that we can avoid the same fate. We can keep at bay the potential random chaos pressing against the limits of our ordered existence. Reasons, we think, protect us from the dark forces of the world. After being raped in a parking lot at night, victims prefer to reason, "It was my fault. I was raped because I wore my skirt too short, or I fumbled too long trying to get my key out of my purse, or because I didn't take that karate class I intended," rather than, "I am a victim of random violence." Finding causes sustains the illusion that we might, after all, have been in control had we made different choices.

Finally, we search for answers because we think that a meal of reasons will fill us up. If we can just pinpoint that determining cause, we will be satisfied.

Here's the way this search process works. A ten-year-old boy develops brain cancer. The parents, flailing in grief, turn the storehouse of reasons upside down looking for something they can take away for comfort. The child is too young to have wrecked his body through drinking, smoking, bad food habits, or drugs. None of those reasons fit. Was the child under undue stress and unable to express it? No. Family history finally reveals that obscure great-uncle Joe also died of a brain tumor. Aha! The reason! The tendency to get cancer can be an inherited disease, and the young boy possibly fell heir to faulty DNA. Thin, but better than nothing.

The only problem is that the answer does not satisfy or comfort the parents. They continue to batter heaven because they realize that there is a deeper "why?" still unanswered. Their initial question "why?" has been dealt with in worldly terms, but the reason given doesn't answer the real question.

As humans we live in the world, and when evil touches us personally in one of its myriad possible ways—from cancer, to murder, to rape, to divorce, to a train wreck—our first temptation is to seek an answer from the world. Believers and nonbelievers alike scrounge the field, looking for satisfaction, for a sense of power over the event. Then, whether we find a legitimate cause or not, we realize we still hunger for a deeper answer. We have combed the material world for tangible answers, but "Why?" is a spiritual question.

Once we realize we've fooled ourselves into thinking that answers will quell the longing, our search enters a new realm. Job, the quintessential biblical questioner, senses from the first that he will not find an earthly reason for his suffering. He sits in his backyard among the ashes scraping his scabs with a potsherd, enduring the cynicism of his wife and the foolishness of his friends. He knows he has not done anything to deserve his fate, though his friends suggest that there must be a reason for his calamity. Job desires to go directly to God and say, "Do not condemn me; let me know why thou dost contend against me" (10:2).

"Why?" becomes a battle cry, a challenge to the Almighty. We don't want literal, physical reasons why something happened, but rather we want to know why God has allowed it to happen.

THE WORLD'S UNDERSTANDING

In Martin Luther's hymn "A Mighty Fortress Is Our God," verse three speaks of the world as being filled with devils and ruled by the "prince of darkness grim." However, we need not fear or tremble before these forces, because one word, *Jesus,* dispels their power. Set to Bach's music this hymn is a rousing triumph over the world's potential for destruction.

There are two truths we need to laminate on 3 x 5 cards and keep with us at all times. One, the world can be a harmful place. We cannot expect to find perfection here. Two, we will not drown in the quicksand of the world's evil because Jesus Christ is the rope that pulls us out to a place of safety, either on this side of Jordan's bank or sometimes on the opposite shore. Either way, He is our lifeline.

If we start with the proposition that the world can be a harmful place, we will not be so taken aback when evil flattens our noses. Though God is more powerful than the evil one, the prince of darkness has a hand in earthly events. Satan's part of the earthly garden is permeated with canker and blight and tilled by ruthless, avaricious gardeners. Unfortunately, God's and Satan's crops grow side by side, and though we may wish that all evil were walled off in a faraway place, instead the wheat and tares intermingle—both because of our own potential for personal evil and because the world itself is a mixed place.

Evil happens here. We must accept this as a given. And Christians are not exempt. God permits bad things to happen to good people because He has allowed free will all over the planet, and people—including, unfortunately, ourselves—do not always make choices for health, happiness, and the well-being of others.

Evil operates everywhere, ranging in destruction from hurt feelings to the atomic bomb. Fourth grade, I'm finding to my great dismay, is sometimes a dog-eat-dog world among little boys. One boy slyly opened the locker right above another child's head, then fell on the ground laughing when the child conked his crown, nearly sustaining a concussion.

Evil. Not drastically destructive, but evil nonetheless. The impulse to do someone else harm. And it only gets worse.

Simply by journeying through this life, we encounter evil. Our bodies sicken and die; others set traps for us; airplanes blow up; we lose our jobs; people we love leave us. We also sabotage our own good intentions and deeds. To demand to understand why these things happen is to ignore the ground rule: God gave us our freedom, and the world is a place where we and others misuse it.

That is the bad news. Now for the good news. Once we realize that the world's answers won't satisfy our spiritual hunger, we turn to God with a different kind of question. "Why?" this time is the beginning of a probe into the nature of God. What kind of a God sets up a world like this? If He's good, then why does He allow Satan in to do his dirty work? Once we turn our search in this direction, we begin, literally, to see the light. We cannot formulate God's answers to these questions in reasonable, ordered arguments, but we can come to a wordless understanding and acceptance of the One who created us in the first place.

Job's determination to ask God Himself "Why?" led not to an answer, but to the revelation of God Himself. In His loving nature, God redeems every single horror, if we let Him. Always getting the last word, God can use evil's worst as the starting place for mercy. After the world hands us a nasty blow, we turn to God, and Satan is powerless. Our prayer is answered thus: "I love you and am with you through this trial." Love fells Satan every time.

Of course life is difficult. Of course we are faced with tragedy. Given this starting place, the good news begins to seep in like light from under the door of our closets of pain. We are not left to suffer alone but are joined by the Spirit of consolation.

For me, this played out that first Christmas after my parents' divorce, the Christmas I had dreaded. Mother greeted us at the door of her new townhouse with, "This house is a happy house!" Instead of weeping in our eggnog, we sat around a live, potted pine tree decorated with the funny, lopsided, spangly ornaments we'd made as children. Mother gave us truckloads of special belongings that didn't fit in her new house, and we laughed giddily as each new/old treasure was unwrapped. Soon we were submerged in a snowbank of discarded wrapping paper. God's grace had won after all.

The temptation to understand the ways of the world sometimes prevents us from allowing the Holy Spirit to bring us comfort in the middle of tribulation. I have listened, heartbroken, to people who refuse to believe in a God who allows babies to be born with defects, a God who allows war, a God who allows the earth to be tilled and sown with a variety of disasters. I, too, have watched the news some evenings nibbling on snacks in my safe home while visions of starving children, war atrocities, murders, crime, and bombings stalk relentlessly across the TV screen, and thought, *God, how can You allow these terrible things? What kind of a world is this?*

Again, the answer is not an answer, but an awareness of God's love calling us to make an affirmation in spite of the evidence. God will conquer this world for good, but not, probably, in the next month or two. In the meantime, it is my place to pray for all those people I see on my TV, to do what I can to help in my tiny corner of the planet, and to trust that God knows what He's doing. If I allow my gall at the world's evil to come between God and me, then I become a silent partner in it. Centuries of philosophers have failed to answer the question of evil adequately. To worship the answer to this one is to miss the point entirely.

COSMIC UNDERSTANDING

When we lived in the Washington, D.C., metro area, I once attended a lecture given by a brilliant scientist who worked on the government's secret team developing the "Star Wars" weaponry. He was an atheist.

With a panorama of visual aids and charts and bold, black-lettered statistics, this man explained (with security clearance, of course) how some of the new weapons functioned in the cosmos. Though his talk was geared for nonscientists, he still didn't simplify enough for me. With a subnormal science IQ, I didn't understand most of his facts. The diagrams looked like space toys for children.

What I remember is the man's brilliance.

The laws of the cosmos have always held a temptation for those intelligent enough to understand them. The power of the universe lures the brightest of our race to attain a

Godlike understanding of the way the planets and galaxies and atoms work. And just as the amount of available scientific information has increased exponentially since Dr. Faustus's time, so has the impulse to know and to control through knowledge. In fact, people today are probably more determined to control through knowledge. Look at the plethora of self-help books. We can explain almost anything. Additionally, much of our expanded knowledge of the universe is not for its own sake, but for the sake of, say, beating the Russians to the moon or waging war and destruction. The potential for evil at the cosmic level staggers the mind.

I am not picking on scientists here. The advancements of science have increased the health and happiness of the human race, and many scientists are devoted Christians. I am talking here about any intellectual endeavor seeking to prove God or His mysteries at the expense of allowing Him into our lives. To prove Him first before accepting Him or to figure out the divine mysteries such as the Incarnation, the Virgin Birth, or the Resurrection before we worship Him is idolatry. The goal of much intellectual pursuit is certainty and power, not God—even if the search is couched in theological terms. We want faith to fit together as neatly as facts do, to force the rules of faith to govern as absolutely as the law of gravity.

For example, one of the most brilliant men I ever met in the field of English literature had devoured the philosphy, criticism, theology, and literature of the last two thousand years, haunted by his search for proof of God's existence. Suggestion wasn't enough. Other peoples' personal testimonies weren't enough. Glimpses of mystery weren't enough. This voracious man wanted proof, pure and simple. Until he found it, he would remain an atheist.

Other examples are the attempts to prove biblical miracles over the last two centuries, the attempt to pin down with scientific certainty Jesus' resurrection, the Jesus Seminar's "voting" to determine which of Jesus' sayings were really His. These conclusions are interesting, perhaps, but dangerous and beside the point, especially if we use the paucity of scientific or scholarly evidence to keep us from believing in Jesus as the Son of God.

A proof-hungry age like ours produces many who cannot let go of the need for certainty. Proof is safe. A person trained to mistrust and discard anything not backed up by documentable data has a difficult time jumping the chasm between what we know and what we don't. However, even in the most holy pursuits, the fact remains: God's creation and His Word can be tested and explained and categorized and manipulated (up to a point), but God Himself cannot.

Since the Renaissance, the relationship between learning and faith has been a rocky one and has led to current postmodern crises in intellectual circles. For centuries, Christians accepted Ptolomy's cosmology and Aristotle's philosophy as scientific proof of the way the universe was created and operated. Then, a series of discoveries threatened the Christian understanding of the perfection of the cosmos.

As Donald G. Dawe so neatly synopsizes in Sewanee's Education for Ministry material, Copernicus discovered that the earth revolved around the sun, not vice versa, thus attacking the biblical observations in Genesis, the Psalms, Ecclesiastes, and Joshua that the sun revolves around the earth. The German astronomer Johann Kepler discovered that the planets move in ellipses, thus wrecking the medieval notion of the perfect circles of planetary orbits as proof of perfection of the divine cosmic order. Galileo's demonstration that gravity acts uniformly on all matter destroyed the medieval understanding of heaven, which was that lighter objects floated up and baser ones sank down. By explaining the motion of heavenly bodies as attracted to one another "directly in proportion to their mass and in inverse proportion to the distance which separates them," Isaac Newton demolished any idea of a heaven of perfection located in space beyond the stars.[2]

These discoveries were made not by atheists seeking to destroy religion, but rather by men trying to understand the nature of the universe. Most of them were condemned by the church—some, like Galileo, to death unless he recanted. We can never go backward to the Middle Ages before the discoveries, when Thomas Aquinas proved the existence of God in terms the culture accepted as real and absolute. Since the Renaissance, we know too much about how the universe works. Oddly enough, today scientific discoveries of the Renaissance have become part of the worldview of Christians. We have recognized that faith and science are two separate realms of inquiry, and to confuse the two jeopardizes the truth of each.

Interestingly, a movement among scientists, especially among quantum physicists, to incorporate prayer and religion is actually moving us from atheism into a reverence for God. Larry Dossey says,

> No one can read accounts of [Einstein's] life and not be struck by the sense of holiness with which he regarded all of creation. Physics was for him no dull affair; it was an attempt to understand God's work. Einstein's theology and his science were tied hand-in-glove; that they could exist separately seemed unthinkable to him.[3]

We still face two temptations, however: first, to apply the methods of science to questions of faith, and second, to reject the need for humility. Like Faustus, we live in an arrogant age. We think we can track the truth, ignoring the paradox that it is the truth that catches us. We can dig and probe and strain until our eyes burn out, but the Eureka moments—the moments of deep aha! when a sliver of light enters the dark, searching soul—are gifts. Our wills and our minds cannot force understanding. Letting go remains essential.

The more we know, the more we want to know; the quest is endless and the rewards titillating. However, ultimately everyone, even the most brilliant human beings, arrive at the chasm: We either lunge in the dark, or not.

THE BAPTISMAL COVENANT

At the bottom, our quest for understanding takes us right back to the Garden of Eden. What we demand is a God-like knowledge of good and evil—especially why an all-good, all-powerful being allows evil to work in the world.

Theologians for millennia have massaged the problem of good and evil in language so lofty and thought so convoluted that I can barely follow their reasoning. In all my reading, I have never found a truly satisfactory answer. Every generation explores this problem as if, finally, our finite minds will grasp the essentially ungraspable. It can't be done. Like oil rigs built far out into the Atlantic, these arguments float on the vast ocean of the mystery of God.

I am not suggesting we shouldn't try to understand God's ways. To throw up our hands and say, "Oh, well. It's a mystery. I'm not going to waste my time thinking about it" can stunt our spiritual growth, whereas prayerfully pondering the mystery of God can lead to spiritual riches. No, I am saying that our need to understand God shouldn't become a barrier against experiencing His love. At the experiential level, only one thing matters: God comes to us in our pain, our joy, our bewilderment. We experience God firsthand when we hear Him speak to us through the Holy Spirit, "I love you. It's going to be all right. I am with you. You can endure this trial."

The Baptismal Covenant in the Episcopal Church asks the candidates to renounce evil at three levels. First, at the cosmic level: "Do you renounce Satan and all the spiritual forces of wickedness that rebel against God?" This question evokes the best answer of the problem of evil (outside the Bible) that I've ever read, found in John Milton's *Paradise Lost,* a self-proclaimed attempt to "justify the ways of God to men."[4] Instead of using a rational, rhetorical argument, Milton simply gives us the picture of Satan choosing hell over heaven, choosing his own self-sufficiency and unbridled ambition over the love of God. As a result, we see God hurling Satan headlong, in flames, falling hideously into hell. The principle of free will extends to the levels of creation above our own. The angels, too, choose to be either near God or in hell. As a result, the potential for evil infiltrates the universe, not because God is powerless to stop it, but because He loves His creatures—all of them—so much that He gives even His angels the choice.

The second question for the baptismal candidates reads: "Do you renounce the evil powers of this world which corrupt and destroy the creatures of God?" This question recognizes the forces of collective evil, like famine, racism, war, waste, pollution—evils we participate in merely because we exist as members of the human race on earth. Systemic evil invades our lives from politics to family dynamics. The third question, "Do you renounce all sinful desires that draw you from the love of God?" deals with evil at the personal level, our own evil, the personal desires and inclinations we'd rather hide from than face.

Our job as Christians is not to try to explain evil. It is a nugget of darkness impossible to crack. More importantly, once "explained," we take the attitude that evil is no longer evil but merely a social disease, a psychological problem, a mistake in judgment. No, evil is best recognized for what it is, and renounced.

In summary, the desire to grow in the knowledge and love of God is a good and righteous prayer. As St. Augustine said, "Understanding is the reward of faith. Therefore seek not to understand that thou mayest believe, but believe that thou mayest understand." Understanding becomes an idol only when our desire to know becomes greater than our desire for God.

God's answer to "Whys?" is always "I love you." That is all we really need to know.

Chapter 11

LIFE

For whoever would save his life
will lose it; and whoever loses his life for
my sake and the gospel's will save it.

—MARK 8:35

As soon as her mother left with Aunt Dot for the mall, Patty started egging on her cousin, Maggie. "C'mon. Just let me take it down to the end of the street. Nobody will ever know." Patty gazed longingly at her aunt's burnt orange Mercedes convertible sports coupe, dazzling in the sunlight of the driveway, keys already in the ignition. "Don't be such a dork."

Maggie twined her finger around a strand of loose hair near her ear. She said slowly, "Mom would kill me if she found out." She hesitated just a second too long for her daredevil cousin.

Patty jumped in the driver's seat. "But she's never going to find out, is she? Get in."

"You're not even fifteen yet. You don't even have a learner's permit." Maggie tossed the strand of hair back over her shoulder.

Patty turned the ignition. "This is one sweet car. Get in before I back it over your shoes."

Reluctantly, Maggie opened the door and sat down. Neither girl buckled her seat belt. "Just to the stop sign. Promise?"

Patty put the car in reverse and varoomed out the driveway, shifting gears like a race car driver and speeding down the street. Maggie's hair streamed forward, in her face. As she pulled a ropy strand out of her mouth and away from her eyes, she screamed, "Look out!" A moving van had made a wide turn at the corner and blocked the intersection.

Patty hit the accelerator instead of the brake by mistake.

On impact, she was thrown clear of the wreckage, fracturing her wrist. Maggie, on the other hand, broke her neck and smashed her skull against the side of the truck.

A neighbor, Mrs. Scott, had known both girls since their mothers strolled them as babies around the block. Watering the African violets in her living room, she saw the accident, called 911, and flew hysterically out of her house. Kneeling beside Maggie, unconscious and dying near the curb, Mrs. Scott prayed over and over, "Lord, please let this child live. Please let her live."

Two years later, Maggie's parents made the painful decision to move her to the state facility. They had tried to keep her at home; they had transformed their den into a hospital room and hired nurses around the clock. Maggie was incontinent. She never regained consciousness, although her eyelids flickered occasionally.

Maggie's parents and Mrs. Scott remembered the moment of decision when they allowed the EMS team to revive her from death to life. *From death to life,* Mrs. Scott often thought ironically. *Didn't they get it backward, wooing her soul from everlasting life back to a deathlike state of existence?* After two years, Maggie was almost brain-dead, yet her heart continued to beat, thanks to her curbside revival by EMS and modern technology. Maggie's parents were bankrupt, on the brink of divorce. Patty had been in counseling for two years and had tried to commit suicide.

Life.

Mrs. Scott wondered occasionally deep in the night if she had prayed the wrong prayer. Maybe praying that Maggie be taken home to heaven would have been a more loving request.

LIFE AND DEATH

Until I sat down to write this chapter, I had never really examined closely my definition of life, with all the hidden, embedded conditions for its quality. The New Testament sharply divides references to "life" into two categories, earthly life and life everlasting, and they are two separate, different entities. Though, according to John, eternal life begins now, it is fulfilled after death. Preceding the next life, this life influences the quality of the next. For example, the beggar Lazarus suffers greatly in his earthly life but is rewarded in the next, while the tightwad rich man burns in eternity after an earthly life of luxury and indifference to the suffering of the poor. How each man acted in this life determined how they spent eternal life. Whether we accept Christ in this life or not determines how we will spend eternity.

In all four gospels, to confuse the value of earthly life and everlasting life is deadly. Luke reminds his readers of Lot's wife, who wanted to hang on to what she had. "Whoever seeks to gain his life will lose it, but whoever loses his life will preserve it" (17:33). Life as we know it in our raggedy flesh and earthly hankerings is not the important part, and to scramble for the crumbs this life offers us is to miss out on the big feast later.

Our culture tells us the opposite. Carpe diem. Seize the day. This is all you're gonna get baby, so grab for the big one.

Christians must find a way to live with one foot in both worlds. We are not called to lock ourselves away and wait passively to die so that we can save ourselves for the big prize later. Even most twentieth-century monastic orders are actively involved in some facet of this life. Monks from

Conception, Missouri, make and sell beautiful greeting cards; other monastic orders offer spiritual direction and retreats; and an order of sisters near Brenham, Texas, breeds miniature horses, and a barefoot nun shows visitors the tiny pet-like, dog-sized animals. As the song says, you can meet the saints of God anywhere, finding them "in school, or in lanes, or at sea, in church, or in trains, or in shops, or at tea."[1] They are busy making this life better and loving those around them. Salvation is a this-world event. In fact, this world is so important that God took on our flesh and pitched His tent on our shores, traveling around Galilee awhile in skin just like ours.

At the same time, we need to remember that our existence on earth is not the be all and end all. When we become enmeshed in our lives, losing sight of the other dimension, we

> are half-hearted creatures, fooling about with drink
> and sex and ambition when infinite joy is offered us,
> like an ignorant child who wants to go on making
> mud pies in a slum because he cannot imagine what
> is meant by the offer of a holiday at the sea. We are
> far too easily pleased.[2]

In other words, when we place too much emphasis on the pleasures of being alive in this world, we have been seduced by a lesser god.

Roget's *Thesaurus* gives several synonyms for the word

life, among them "survival," "vitality," "animation," "existence," "longevity," "being," and "essence," each providing a slightly different shade of meaning. I'd like to look at each of these in terms of both earthly life and everlasting life to see how we sometimes become overly enamored of this world, forgetting that the choice is not between life and death, but between life and life.

SURVIVAL

Survival implies life, after some sort of threat to life. The very word contains the notion that life has continued or endured over and above adversity. One of the popular genres for TV shows and movies is reflected in the new series "I Survived a Disaster" (the disaster being an earthquake, asteroid, twister, volcano, avalanche, alien attack, you name it). We in the audience sit in our recliners clutching our soft drinks, gripped by the question, "How will the hero—with whom we have all identified—survive?"

Watching survivors from the comfort of an easy chair is very different from surviving personally. My sister and brother-in-law witnessed a car careening over a bridge into the water. They stopped and pulled the driver out of the sinking car. The experience of participating in a heroic survival episode required some deep examination of the questions we don't ask when it's the movie stars who emerge unscathed.

216

When I was fourteen, my family went skiing in Colorado over Christmas. At the end of the day—twilight settling over the mountains like a dusting of snow—we packed up and headed over Monarch Pass. Though my father was driving carefully on the winding road, suddenly the car started to slide like a toy backward toward the edge of the mountain. In one split second, we knew we were heading toward oblivion unless a miracle happened.

The miracle was a six-inch strip of gravel at the very edge of the road, where the road disappeared straight down the mountain. With the end of our station wagon hanging off the side of the pass, we gingerly crawled out the front of the car, hearts pounding when we saw how near we had come to death.

Why? Why had we been spared? This question has lingered with me over the years. Surviving a near-tragedy has left me humbled and grateful—and scarred. To this day, I am irrationally miserable climbing up a mountain road. My husband had to let me out of the car halfway up Pike's Peak two years ago because I simply couldn't bear the ride.

On the one hand, our country worships survivors. Survivors on the news are heroes. Whether they start out famous or just folks like us, by the end of the show, they are surrounded by the press because they have done the impossible. They have the right combination of brains, instinct, and luck to beat tremendous odds.

God seems to bless survivors. The other poor people in

the movie or the news show who were crushed, drowned, zapped, or blown away were not blessed. In the Old Testament equation (prosperity equals the Lord's blessing), survivors wear God's special mark of approval.

On the other hand, for those of us who have survived a near-death experience, important questions haunt us. Yes, we are blessed. No question. However, why weren't others blessed, too? I will never forget watching the news coverage of the Air Florida crash in the Potomac River. One man struggled to save the life of a young girl, then drowned himself. Why? Is survival random? Is God up there drawing lots? Who will live and who will not?

No doubt about it, survivors are changed by the experience. Even on shallow TV shows, the characters usually metamorphose into deeper, more insightful people. For example, in the movie Twister, the couple rediscovers that they love each other in the aftermath of the storm. Survival brings with it wisdom.

Survival also brings with it more life as we know it. We get to stay in our familiar world instead of dying into another place which is undoubtedly better—but we don't know for sure. Heaven sounds great, but maybe we don't want to be whisked away with no warning. Earthly life has a comfortable familiarity about it, and why rush things? Eternity is, after all, a long time.

What about Maggie, who "survived" the car crash only in the technical sense that her body was living through the experience? The artificial resuscitation in her case left her without life in any real, meaningful sense—at least as we can measure and understand it. But who's to say? Perhaps Maggie's soul rests in a place of peace and beauty deeper than the souls of the rest of us, souls enmeshed with mobile bodies and frenetic brain cell activity.

The point is, whether we live or whether we die, we belong to the Lord, and our survival in this life and the next is in His loving hands.

VITALITY

Remember the cheesecake shots of beauties like Farrah Fawcett and Jane Fonda that appeared on magazine covers when they turned fifty? I personally never looked that good at twenty, but these women never stopped representing the image of vitality, long after their youth.

Connotations of the word *vitality* include health, vigor, force, power, beauty; images of Wheaties champions, super athletes, and robust long-distance runners come to mind. Vitality is life defined by good health, proper exercise, correct diet, and plenty of sleep.

An ad on TV shows an older couple, bursting with vitality, saying, "We may not have much, but we have our health. That's just about everything." Vitality is easy to worship because we are so eager to avoid its opposites: lethargy, pain, depression.

As a culture, we tend to worship health and vitality in one of two ways. The first is obvious, measured by the sheer number of dollars we spend on health clubs, personal trainers, equipment, vitamins, herbs, and products to make our hair shine, our bodies trim. The covers of our magazines give us the goal to shoot for: Never mind that most of us fall short. Pain-free beauty is still the idol. We stock our cabinets with drugs to keep us well, to take away headaches, to calm upset stomachs, to ease arthritis. We undergo liposuction, we drink smoothies instead of milkshakes for lunch, we diet constantly—all in homage to the god of vitality and vanity.

The downside of obsession with vitality includes problems like bulimia, anorexia, and drug addiction. The god of vitality can actually lead us into a death trap. The more we focus on how we look and feel, the less likely we are to focus on the true giver of vitality. If we focus on God, we are more likely to keep our health and our looks in balance.

Teresa had an obsessive friend who invited her over to lunch on occasion. Teresa dreaded these lunches. "From the moment I walk in the door, every item on the menu is analyzed. This person cannot talk about anything but caloric, fat, sugar, or salt intake. Lunch with her is not a time to share companionship but an opportunity to worry whether the one gram of fat left in baked tortilla chips will ruin the afternoon."

Taking care of one's health is not a bad goal, of course.

Our bodies are temples of the Holy Spirit, and I know that my body feels better and responds more readily to life in general when it isn't packed with the globules of fat that tend to cling to my stomach when I eat too much and don't exercise. I am basically too lazy and too poor to be a proper health goddess—however, the temptation to become consumed with this aspect of vitality lies in wait for all of us interested in our health. Balance is the secret.

Another way our culture worships vitality and health is less obvious, but just as obsessive. When I was growing up, an old lady in town ruled her household from her bed. She'd been sickly since I could remember. People said, "Oh, yes. Mrs. X. She's enjoyed poor health for years." Even as a child, the paradoxical phrase "enjoyed poor health" struck me. Who in their right mind would enjoy being sick? I didn't yet understand the power that comes with a disease augmented by imagination. I hadn't learned how one can milk a chic minor ailment. At our house, when we were sick, we took nasty medicine, got shots, and stayed in bed without TV As a result of no excess pampering, we were seldom psychosomatically ill. I have always been grateful for the way my family handled illness.

British novelist Charles Dickens wrote many novels with vivid and sometimes startling characters. One such character is Miss Haversham in *Great Expectations*. Disappointed by love, she shut herself up with her bridal array and literally shriveled.

I saw that the bride within the bride dress had withered like the dress. Once, I had been taken to one of our old marsh churches to see a skeleton in the ashes of a rich dress that had been dugout of a vault under the church pavement. Now, wax-work and skeleton seemed to have dark eyes that moved and looked at me.[3]

Emotionally and physically debilitated, Miss Haversham was nonetheless one of the most powerful and controlling people in town. Victorian literature is filled with all sorts of women who gain attention and power through fainting in dramatic swoons.

A woman I'll call Randee is the American twentieth-century counterpart to the Victorian heroine. She reads all the latest medical journals and suffers from most of the major chic ailments like chronic fatigue syndrome, mitral valve prolapse, and adult attention deficit disorder. Like fashions in clothes, illnesses parade through medical journals and emerge in pop magazines, becoming available to anyone who is chronically tired or needing attention. I am not talking about people who really have these illnesses; I'm talking about the fixation on health manifested by an overabsorption with current, trendy illness. We worship, in reverse, the god of vitality when we use poor health to gain attention and power.

Illness is part of being alive. Speaking personally, I hate to be sick, but I know that God speaks to me through illness. The loss of vitality can be a way for us to lift our eyes off the state of our bodies onto the Creator, who knows us better than any doctor. During my daughter's first year of life, together we caught at least a dozen colds. I have never been so weary, exhausted, miserable—and as I rocked my sniffling, coughing baby, I prayed she would not suffer like this the rest of her life.

God spoke to me in those months of illness. He reminded me that sickness is a condition of humanness. He assuaged my guilt for helplessly succumbing time and time again to that first faint tickle in the back of the throat. He loved me even though I complained so much. Eventually, He brought us both out of the long stint of sickness.

During that year, it was difficult not to focus on my daughter's and my illness. Lifting my eyes to God required discipline and endurance. Coming from a background of health made it all the more difficult not to obsess about being sick. I learned what a trap it was to worship vitality. We can eat properly; we can exercise every day and get plenty of sleep; we can get regular check-ups; but health, like grace, is a gift.

We are not promised health and vitality, but we are promised the presence of God—even on a sickbed. In the long run, vitality is exactly what we must all sacrifice to die into a life even more exciting than any health club can offer.

ANIMATION AND EXISTENCE

I love the word *animation* because it has so many connotations. The "coming alive" of the Seven Dwarfs, for instance, or any of Disney's fantastic creations, suggests a miracle: From the thin air of the artist's imagination and pieces of flat paper, characters leap and cavort in our minds for the rest of our lives after seeing the "animation" of films such as *Snow White*.

Animation also brings to mind a barnyard, with the smell of fresh hay, mud, and oats. Animals share a common root word—as fellow creatures breathing air to get their necessary elements like oxygen instead of using the process of photosynthesis like plants. *Animation* shouts of enthusiasm and exhilaration. I can almost hear life-giving wind *(anima)* blowing through the word, and it reminds me of the Holy Spirit.

For me, the Holy Spirit is the key difference in the contrast between an animated life and mere existence.

The current trend of postmodernism emphasizes meaninglessness, despair, disunity, fragmentation, and loss of center. This nihilistic worldview has permeated everyday life to a certain degree and runs counter to the Christian message. In spite of this lifeless outlook, people who buy into this philosophy manage to live long lives and often have productive careers as teachers and writers (though a "productive" career itself contradicts their creed). Wayne Booth, at the beginning of postmodernism, rightly pegged the correct response to such negative thinking. He said, "For the complete nihilist, suicide, not the creation of significant forms, is the only consistent gesture."[4] Any nihilistic writer contradicts his or her own philosophy the minute pen is put to paper.

Postmodernists and other nihilists exist rather than live. They wake up in the morning like the rest of us, hungry and looking for something to do. Their activities, however—if they live according to what they profess—do not fill them with joy or meaning. Their lives stand for nothing except personal interest, and their beliefs do not extend beyond acquisition or other forms of pleasure. They procreate, raise children, die. Simple existence is the formula for their lives.

Over and against this depressing view, Christianity offers us animation. Christ weaves meaning into the random strands of personal events. Our lives form a story, not just senseless babble, and this story ties in with the larger story of the people of God. Meaning is one of the great gifts of Christianity.

Hope is another gift that animates our lives—the comfort of the Holy Spirit in the dark of night, knowing that the searing pain of loss or the exhaustion of despair will not win in the long run.

Once I charted my spiritual life. When I finished it looked like an outline of the front range of the Rocky Mountains. Highs included my initial conversion experience, the moment Stockton and I first looked into the faces of our children—my son, his face furled in sleep, and my daughter, who flashed us dimples like tiny grape seeds. God was overwhelmingly present in those moments. Or, at seminary my first year. Nine months of peaks decorated the chart at that point in my life.

Then there are the valleys. My brother-in-law's slow decline and death from cancer. The murder of my relatives. Not finding a job for several years. God slid behind giant, towering, black thunderstorm clouds that filled the sky during those periods.

Personally, I love the highs, the times of special animation when the Holy Spirit seems to breathe life into my soul. My temptation is to worship the religious highs, to seek peak experiences, to cling to the rocks on the mountaintop, instead of acknowledging that the valleys are as much a part of the Christian life as the highs.

Jesus also lives in the valley. The valley is where He teaches us. Even in His earthly life, He did not stay up on the Mount of Transfiguration but came down the hill to work. The highs are the fireworks; He grows us up in the valley.

Sometimes, the Christian life is neither high nor low but simply becomes overcast and loses its color. Fortunately, Christians have a gift even in the fog of depression. As we breathe in the air around us, we also breathe in the presence of the Holy Spirit. Many nights I have spent wrestling with deep spiritual issues, wondering if the joie de vivre I used to feel would ever return, or if I would simply slug out the rest of my days in a blue funk. The great gift of animation comes at first as a tiny, tiny spark of hope, almost imperceptible.

Then, with prayer and endurance, it grows into a larger fire. Jesus never promises that we won't have days when we feel we only exist. Yet He does promise that He will send the Holy Spirit to bring us back to life.

LONGEVITY

My older sibling died before he or she was finished being formed in my mother's womb. A friend's son died before he could talk, a limp little body with a brain tumor, buried finally in a tiny coffin. The death of children always pulls at my heart. They seem so cheated of life.

The Bible talks about the normal life span as three score and ten—seventy years. Growing up, we expect to live until old age; we don't expect our lives to be truncated by car wrecks, murder, cancer, accidents. When someone we know dies suddenly or prematurely, we experience, along with the loss, a keen sense that they were gypped out of something they deserved.

In the last several years, I have developed a different view of life and longevity. Everyone on the planet who woke up this morning is on equal footing. We have each been given one day. Period. Some of us may not make it until noon. Others won't make it until supper, and others won't last the night. The rest of us will wake up tomorrow and be given one more day.

I'm sure it irritates my children when, on the way to

school, especially when the sun shines brightly and the birds are singing, I exclaim, "Hey, kids, guess what! God has given us another day!" Yeah, right, Mom. But I'm serious. Not only have I learned to be exquisitely grateful for another day, but I've become exquisitely aware that it may be the last one I ever get.

Living like this (when I remember to—instead of worrying about what I'm going to do next fall, or where we're going to live when we retire) keeps me from worshiping the fickle god of longevity. I may not get my three score and ten years. On the other hand, most of the women in my family have lived well into their nineties, and I may get to dandle my great-grandchildren on my knee. I hope I get to live lots and lots and lots more, but since I don't know what God has in store for me, I try to keep my eyes focused on the only moment I'm guaranteed: this one.

Jesus did not get a long life in our terms. Dying at thirty-three seems in this day and age like a crime and a waste of life. God's economy doesn't jive with either our reason or our hopes. The older I get, the less I understand about why in the heck we're here on the face of this earth in the first place—some of us in relatively easy lives, others in poverty and hardship; some of us for very short periods of time, and others for a hundred years. God knows, and has His purposes, but I get more and more clueless the more I witness the apparently senseless waste of life.

The news last night showed a young local man on trial

for the murder of a nine-month-old baby. "Why? Why? Why?" I asked in outrage. Why was this young life taken? I don't know. God judges the value and the longevity of life with different scales, and somehow He is in charge, in spite of the inequities.

We must live in trust—and gratitude—for one more day.

ESSENCE AND BEING

When I was a teenager, somebody gave me a green and gold-leaf Florentine tray, and I started keeping my perfume bottles on it. Today, the tray adorns my dresser, crowned with bottles of all shapes, sizes, and scents. I call it my memory tray because one whiff from each bottle, and an entire era is brought back. For example, a quick spray from Polo brings back the summer in Austin when it rained so much that mold started to grow on the walls, when the trees and grass grew lush and deep. A splash of Yardley brings back castles in Wales and the little café where we had tea and scones and heard, of all things, "Ghost Riders in the Sky."

One sniff, and I'm transported back in time. The essence of an experience is recalled in a few drops of scent collected on a gold-leaf tray on my dresser.

Essence and being are what we take with us from this life to the next.

Each of us has an essence, something identifiable and uniquely us—the "you-ness" and the "me-ness" we come to know through hanging around with each other. Almost like a particular lingering scent, our essence shines through, for example, in the friend who manages to send a heart-warming note just when we're blue. "Isn't that just like Mary?" we say. Or the brother who cracks a joke at a moment of tension. As friends and relations, we only get glimpses of another's essence, through mannerisms, conversation, and what overflows in daily interchanges.

Essence and being are what God gives us the moment of conception. Boom—we are infused with being. This essence is what we give back to Him when we decide to follow Him as Lord.

The difference between what He gives us and what we give Him is that His gift of life is total and immediate. Giving back our essence to God is more complicated, and takes us most of the rest of our lives.

I gave my life to Jesus one afternoon in a pink shower stall, where I'd been crying for so long that the water had turned cold. That moment marked my conversion, and I gave Christ as much of me as I understood. Almost immediately, I experienced a hunger to know more about Christ and the Bible, so I signed up for the Bethel Bible class at church. The more I studied the Word of God, the more understanding I received about my Lord, and about my life. As I traveled down the path of faith, light helped me find whole new pieces of my personality and parts of my past that I also needed to give to Christ.

Since that day twenty years ago, I have grown and developed into a very different person from that young girl who'd driven her life right into a pink shower stall. But I'm not finished yet. Every time I wrestle spiritually, or feel God teaching me something else I need to know, another part of me grows and emerges—and needs to be given back to God.

Who we are—our essence—is like a bulb. With our conception, this bulb is planted in the soil of the earth, where it blooms and blooms during our life span. As each new flower emerges, we give it back to our Creator. Then, when death cuts all the greenery away, God re-plants the bulb in the new soil of another dimension, but the bulb continues to bloom.

What happens when we try to hold onto our lives, keeping ourselves for ourselves, is that the entire plant becomes stunted and the blooms become fewer. The more we grasp at our own being, the less God can work in us and through us. Letting go is not easy. But trying to cling to ourselves brings with it the loss of real life in its fullness and the chance to grow in Christ for eternity.

So, life in all its definitions, "survival," "longevity," "existence," "animation," "essence," and "being," is a gift from God. We do not create ourselves. We cannot force the earth to sustain us for one extra day outside the will of God. Life is technically a heartbeat, a brainwave; life is also communion for eternity with the one God of the universe. We choose it best when we give it back to the One who gave it to us in the first place.

Chapter 12

DESIRE AND REDEMPTION

*The tragedy of human spiritual life,
according to [Paul] Tillich, is our constant
substitution of realities that we make,
shape, and control for the true God.*

—DONALD DAWE

When I was seven, my mother loaded my sisters and me in the back of Bessie, our rattling, shimmying hulk of a station wagon, and took us to visit a new friend. My mother went into the kitchen to chat over coffee, leaving us in a strange living room, to be entertained by a pack of little boys under the age of ten. Four or five of them with crew cuts hooted, shot, fought, screamed, and rode the arms of the furniture like horses along with the cowboys on the western show flickering from the black-and-white TV in the center of the room. After a few token pistol shots, I retreated to the corner of the couch, wishing I were still young enough to suck my thumb.

At the station break, a commercial for perfume came on. The noise and action stopped dead as those boys stared at the television, gasping audibly in shock. I looked more keenly at the ad, thinking I must have missed something. A woman danced alluringly in evening clothes surrounded by puffs of vapor, and on the screen a small perfume bottle appeared, labeled "My Sin."

One of the older boys ran into the kitchen. "Mom, they had my sin on TV!" Being Episcopalian and not good Roman Catholics as these boys were (and therefore having had no catechism and little Bible training), I had to ask my mother on the way home what kind of perfume was sin that it could disrupt the momentum of a good shoot-out.

I don't remember what my mother said, but I do remember the tremendous power this three-letter word had on those little boys—the power to hush, to enthrall, in effect, to make silent hostages of the cowboys and wild Indians previously wearing out the living room furniture. So, between the commercial itself and its effect, I knew early on that sin was a real showstopper: something secret and deep, something so alluring you can't resist it, something vaporous and hard to pin down, something half-obscured, half-revealed by its surrounding aura—and something very costly.

TRADITIONAL CATEGORIES OF SIN

We all carry around with us a particular definition or sense of sin we have worked out for ourselves, concocted from our backgrounds, our biblical understanding, our church teaching—whether it's theologically accurate or not. A regal, churchgoing, eighty-five-year-old matriarch once stared down a theologian when he suggested that sin was a universal condition of humanness. Steely-eyed, she retorted, "I haven't sinned in sixty years," her neck muscles pulled tight under the loose skin, her white gloves buttoned close at the wrists. According to her own personal definition of sin, she was probably right. Sixty years ago, she had most likely boiled her sin checklist down to the Ten Commandments, and indeed, she had not consciously lied, stolen, or committed adultery since.

The most interesting biographies are written about those wild and woolly people who sinned flagrantly before coming to Christ. Augustine begged to be made holy—but not yet; he was having a hard time giving up his mistress. John Newton wrote "Amazing Grace" after his conversion from slave trading. John Donne led a thrilling life of sexual and political intrigue before his conversion. As a result, his biographer said that when he preached, he spoke as one who knew through experience

> the slipperiness of habitual sin; the merry sins; the laugh-
> ing sins that become crying sins; the whispering sins
> that we rock in our hearts, tossing and tumbling them

in our imaginations; the forgotten sins; the unconsidered, unconfessed, unrepentent sins and all the sins that we call small: enough lascivious glances to make up an adultery, enough covetous wishes for a robbery, enough angry words for a murder.[1]

These people had a keen sense of salvation: They knew precisely the deadliness of that from which they had been saved. American Christians are not all so lucky. Many of us have a vague sense of gratitude because we have a vague sense of sin.

Sin is the substitution of self-interest for God at the core of our being, and this form of self-interest is what idolatry is all about. Eve wanted that apple and the wisdom it represented more than she wanted God's will. In the center of her being, she desired to know as much as God. She wanted the ability to discern between good and evil. She wanted her eyes to be opened. She wanted all these things more than she wanted to follow what God had told her to do (or rather, not to do). In essence, Eve worshiped knowledge more than God.

We are tempted at many levels to replace God and His will with whatever it is we want most at the time. When I was a teenager, I thought I would die if I didn't get asked out on a date by a certain boy. When I was older, I thought I'd die if I didn't get to have children. Later, I thought I'd die if I didn't get a particular job.

The key phrase here is "I thought I'd die." Crafty as

ever, Satan always presents sin to us as life. Temptation weasles in with its act of trick mirrors and holds up to us reflections of light, goodness, sustenance, peace, and other things we think we can't live without. The alternative seems drab, even destructive, in comparison. Eve's life in the Garden probably seemed boring after the scintillating possibility of being as smart as God. When we take over and cling to a goal, even a worthy goal such as a determination to do church work, we often find ourselves in trouble.

God's gifts such as goodness, security, love, life, fulfillment, or ministry seduce us into believing they, not God, are the source of light and life. However, these aren't the only possibilities. Without much effort, I find myself sliding right into worshiping almost anything—my children, my husband, my job, self-reliance, worth, painlessness, and so on. Because of free will, I can choose to worship God, or things less than God. My soul seems unavoidably attracted to all sorts of lesser gods; but with God's gift of love and grace, I can also choose to set my course toward Him.

This is the human situation. All our efforts to crawl, hide from, or ascend out of this condition are futile. Like the tragic, ironic piece of wreckage pulled from the ocean after the Challenger exploded, with the word *rescue* painted on the side and an arrow pointing toward a useless hatch, we cannot save ourselves.

Fortunately, this is not the end of the story.

THE GIFT OF REDEMPTION

Picture this life. You live in a lush landscape with bougain-villeas and gardenias delighting the eye and filling the air with perfume. No weeds clog your gardens. Banana trees, canteloupe, asparagus, oranges, strawberries—all your fa-vorite foods grow within walking distance of your front door. You suffer no grocery lines, no floods, no droughts, no traffic.

You have the perfect job. No overtime. No hassles. Your spouse always understands you. Recreation is at your fingertips.

Your car never breaks down. You are never exhausted at the end of the day. You never have PMS (or live with some-body who does); and, best of all, every time you look in the mirror, you see a youthful, beautiful face filled with love.

You are not lonely and not crowded. You are fulfilled. You are in a perfect relationship with God. You feel He always listens to you and meets your every need, even be-fore you have to ask.

Then comes the apple, and one teeny bite wrecks the whole set-up, bringing headaches, violence, car wrecks, and death.

The theology works like this: God created us good and we blew it. Humankind lost the Garden; the place of unin-hibited, unhindered communion with God; the place where desires were reasonable and easily fulfilled and where self-interest did not choke the landscape like mangrove vines.

238

Adam and Eve and the rest of us got kicked out of paradise and were sent to live east of Eden, where pain and trials still torment the children of God. But from the first, God has shown mercy. The punishment for eating the wrong fruit was death, but God did not slay Adam and Eve on the spot. Rather, He gave them life, but life limited. He also removed them from the Garden so they couldn't eat from the tree of everlasting life, the other forbidden fruit. East of Eden, death would "free" them from the toil of their limited life.

God never stopped loving His wayward creatures. Plan Number One: God chose a particular people, the Israelites, and to them, God gave the gift of atonement. If they were sorry for their sins, they could sacrifice an animal on the altar and be forgiven. On the Day of Atonement once a year, everybody's sin was placed on the back of a small goat, which was led out into the desert to die.

However, people still didn't get it—they weren't sorry, they forgot about God, they wanted silks and camels and gold bracelets and power instead of faith—so God took stronger measures: He sent His only Son to be the goat. When Jesus died on the cross, once and for all He took the sins of everyone on His body, and these sins killed Him.

This much was predictable: Sin inevitably leads to death.

The surprise was Easter morning. That day probably dawned much like other spring days—light dew on the grass, lilies yawning open, the cemetery gardener poking through moist dirt, at work early to take advantage of the fresh, cool air. Then the women arrived, bearing spices and ointment to prepare Jesus' body properly for burial.

As the women walked toward the mouth of the cave, I'm sure they were experiencing symptoms of grief—disorientation, sleeplessness, that gut-wrenching feeling of loss. They planned to go through the motions of anointment, hoping perhaps that the ritual itself would purge some of their pain in the process.

Imagine the shock of seeing the empty tomb. The glare from the angel alone was probably enough to knock them back a couple of feet. One glance, and the morning was suddenly not like other mornings. The gardener was not the gardener. A new force had been let loose on the earth. The cells of decay had been transformed by new molecular activity into something never before experienced. Jesus' body was beyond description then, and even with all our scientific brilliance, is beyond explanation now.

God had won, after all.

In one weekend long ago, the relationship between God and us changed dramatically. We are no longer stuck with debilitating guilt, waiting until the annual Day of Atonement to send those feelings packing on the back of a small goat. We no longer have to wallow in despair, to cower in unworthiness, to become depressed over the impossible job of trying to be perfect.

God's gift of love and forgiveness means that we don't

240

have to scrounge for scraps of attention or affection; that we can be mulish and stubborn, and God loves us anyway; that we don't have to sip the bitter tea of revenge until we make ourselves sick; that our unfulfilled desires won't kill us in the end; that we can give our second-rate plans to God, and He will sanctify our lives.

Redemption means that the people of God soar above the dust of the earth like an exaltation of larks. The idols of the world grow small and insignificant in the light of God.

With the gift of salvation, God has given us a compass always pointing toward Him. No matter how lost we become, no matter what or who we put in the center of our lives instead of Him, He will always eventually lead us home.

NOTES

Chapter 2—Christian Ministry and Service

1. *Book of Common Prayer.* (New York: Church Hymnal Corporation and Seabury Press, 1979).
2. Lucinda Vardey, ed., *Mother Teresa: A Simple Path.* (New York: Ballantine Books, 1995), xiii.
3. Vardey, xxvi.
4. John Milton, "Sonnet XIX: When I Consider How My Light Is Spent." *Major British Writers,* Vol. 1. G. B. Harrison, ed. (New York: Harcourt, Brace and Co., 1959), 452.

Chapter 3—Security

1. *Book of Common Prayer.*
2. Paul Tillich, *The Shaking of the Foundations.* (New York: Chas. Scribner and Sons, 1948), 161–162.

Chapter 4—Love

1. Richard Garnett, *De Flagelo Myrteo* as quoted by Burton Stevenson in *The Home Book of Quotations Classical and Modern,* Tenth ed. (New York: Dodd, Mead and Co., 1967), 1173.
2. Ralph Waldo Emerson, "Friendship" from *Essays, First Series.* (Boston: Houghton Mifflin & Co., 1903), 212.
3. Stevenson, 1186.
4. Samuel Beckett, *Happy Days* as quoted in *The Bedford Introduction to Drama.* Lee A. Jacobus, ed. (New York: St. Martin's Press, 1989), 815.
5. Alexander Pope, "Eloisa to Abelard" from *The Poems of Alexander Pope.* John Butt, ed. (New Haven: Yale University Press, 1973), 260.

Chapter 5—Urgency

1. Ron DelBene, *The Breath of Life: A Simple Way to Pray.* (Minneapolis, Minn.: Winston Press, 1981), 36.
2. Stephen Covey, *The Seven Habits of Highly Effective People.* (New York: Simon and Schuster, 1989), 145–182.

Chapter 6—Self-Fulfillment

1. Abraham Maslow, as quoted in *Hilgard's Introduction to Psychology.* Rita L. Atkinson, Richard C. Atkinson, and Edward E. Smith, eds. (New York: Harcourt Brace Jovanovich, 1971), 331.
2. Henri J. M. Nouwen, "Door Interview," *The Wittenberg Door.* (Dec./Jan. 1986, Issue No. 88), 19.

Chapter 7—Goodness

1. Dale Hanson Bourke, *Turn Toward the Wind.* (Grand Rapids, Mich.: Zondervan Publishing, 1995), 83.
2. Bourke, 69.
3. Philip P. Hallie, *Lest Innocent Blood Be Shed.* (New York: HarperPerennial, 1979), 69.

Notes

Chapter 8—Worship

1. C. S. Lewis, "The Inner Ring" from *The Weight of Glory*. (Grand Rapids, Mich.: Eerdman's, 1977), 57.
2. Walter Lord, *The Miracle of Dunkirk*. (New York: Viking Press, 1982), 155.

Chapter 9—Ease

1. Joanna Trollope, *The Rector's Wife*. (New York: Random House, 1991), 171.
2. Roberta M. Gilbert, *Extraordinary Relationships: A New Way of Thinking About Human Interactions*. (Minneapolis, Minn.: Chronimed, 1992), 80.
3. Laura Ingalls Wilder, *On the Banks of Plum Creek*. (New York: Harper and Brothers, 1953), 199.
4. Jeanie Wylie-Kellerman, *The Witness*, vol. 79, no. 12, December 1996, 8.
5. Trollope, 107.

Chapter 10—Understanding

1. Christopher Marlowe, "The Tragical History of the Life and Death of Doctor Faustus" from *The Norton Anthology of World Masterpieces*, Vol. 1, Sixth ed. Maynard Mack, ed. (New York: Norton, 1992), Act 1, Scene 1.
2. Donald G. Dawe, *Education for Ministry: Year Four*, Third ed. (Sewanee, Tenn.: University of the South Press, 1992), 155.
3. Larry Dossey, *Recovering the Soul*. (New York: Bantam, 1989), 143.
4. John Milton, *Paradise Lost. Major British Writers*, G. B. Harrison, ed. vol. 1. (New York: Harcourt Brace and Co., 1959), 455.

Chapter 11—Life

1. Isaac Watts, *The Hymnal 1982*. (New York: Church Hymnal Corporation, 1985), 293.
2. C. S. Lewis, *The Weight of Glory*. (Grand Rapids, Mich.: Eerdman's 1977), 2.
3. Charles Dickens, *Great Expectations*, vol. 6. (New York: Peter Fenelon Collier, n.d.), 66.
4. Wayne Booth, *The Rhetoric of Fiction*. (Chicago: University of Chicago Press, 1961), 298.

Chapter 12—Desire and Redemption

1. Elizabeth Gray Vining, *Take Heed of Loving Me.* (Philadelphia: J. B. Lippincott Co., 1964), 5–6.